A Mirror of Medieval Wales

Gerald of Wales and His Journey of 1188

by
Charles Kightly

edited by
David M. Robinson

Cadw: Welsh Historic Monuments
1988

Published by Cadw: Welsh Historic
Monuments, Brunel House,
2 Fitzalan Road, CARDIFF CF2 1UY.

© Cadw: Welsh Historic Monuments

First Published 1988

Designed by Tom Morgan

Typeset by Afal Typesetting

Graphics by Mikeith Design

Printed in Great Britain by
Thamesdown Litho Ltd

ISBN 0 948329 30 0

Cover illustration: *When crusaders vowed to 'take the cross', the expression was no mere metaphor. Cloth crosses were distributed and sewn to their clothing. Here a king receives a cross from a preacher (By permission of the British Library).*

Title page: *An artist's impression of Gerald and Archbishop Baldwin departing from Hereford at the beginning of their mission to Wales (Illustration by Ivan Lapper).*

Frontispiece: *There is no surviving contemporary image of Gerald. This modern statue by Henry Poole is in Cardiff City Hall (By courtesy of Cardiff City Council).*

Contents

Features

Contributors to the Volume

Charles Kightly *(Writer, York)*

R. R. Davies *(Professor of History, University College of Wales, Aberystwyth)*

J. Wyn Evans *(Chaplain, Trinity College, Carmarthen)*

Ralph A. Griffiths *(Professor of Medieval History, University College of Swansea)*

J. M. Lewis *(Formerly Senior Assistant Keeper, National Museum of Wales)*

Huw Pryce *(Department of History, University College of North Wales, Bangor)*

Brynley F. Roberts *(Librarian, National Library of Wales)*

David M. Robinson *(Cadw: Welsh Historic Monuments)*

Glanmor Williams *(Emeritus Professor of History, University College of Swansea, and Chairman of the Ancient Monuments Board for Wales)*

Introduction

Gerald of Wales, *Giraldus Cambrensis,* Gerald the Welshman, *Gerallt Cymro,* he is called: Master Gerald de Barry, Gerald the Marcher, Gerald the Archdeacon, Gerald Bishop-elect of St Davids, he more often called himself. His many names reflect the long and multi-faceted career of one of the most fascinating figures of the Middle Ages. Descended from Norman Marcher barons and Welsh princes, Gerald was by turns scholar, churchman and reformer; courtier, diplomat and would-be crusader; Marcher propagandist, agent of English kings, champion of the Welsh Church, hunted outlaw and cathedral theologian. He was also a naturalist, gossip and indefatigable traveller, but above all a most prolific writer and a tireless self-publicist. From his seventeen surviving books, therefore, we know a great deal about this determined, irascible, self-righteous and utterly fearless man: more, in fact, than about any other inhabitant of early medieval Wales.

Because Gerald was endlessly curious, and almost obsessively anxious to record for posterity the things he discovered, his books also paint a remarkably detailed and wide-ranging picture of medieval Wales itself. Probably the most revealing is his *Journey through Wales,* an account of his eventful tour of the country with Archbishop Baldwin in 1188. He himself called this book, 'a clear mirror, reflecting the wild and trackless places we passed through. It likewise names each spring and rushing river, and records our witty sayings, the hazards of the road, and the various accidents that befell us. It describes the landscape, and the notable things that have happened there both recently and a long time ago, with occasional digressions about natural wonders: and it portrays the country itself, as well as the origins, customs and ways of the inhabitants'.

This present publication retells the story of the journey, setting it in its historical context and against the background of Gerald's varied and turbulent life. It likewise pays particular attention to the many visible traces of Gerald's Wales, traces which help to bring this long vanished man and his land vividly alive today.

An aerial view of St Davids Cathedral and bishop's palace. Gerald's struggle to gain the bishopric was one of the major events in his life. His campaign began in 1176, and only finally ended in 1203.

'The Little Bishop'
Gerald's Family, Childhood and Education

'I am descended from the Princes of Wales and the Barons of the March . . . and I hate to see injustice in either nation'. So declared Gerald during one of the many crises of his life, proclaiming the mixed ancestry which was both his greatest asset and his heaviest burden. Born in about 1146 at Manorbier Castle in Pembrokeshire, the boy we have come to know as 'Gerald of Wales' was in fact three-quarters Norman and a quarter Welsh. His father, William de Barry, came of a family of Norman settlers who took their name

The arms of the de Barry family

from Barry Island near Cardiff, while his mother Angharad was the daughter of the Welsh princess Nest by the famous Norman freebooter Gerald of Windsor — 'a stalwart and cunning man', renowned for his defence of Pembroke Castle.

Most of Gerald's ancestors, then, were 'Barons of the March', the tough Norman 'Marchers' (or 'frontiersmen') who had overrun nearly half of Wales during the decades after the battle of Hastings. Taking advantage of the disunity of the Welsh princes — and with minimum interference from the Norman kings of England — these land-hungry adventurers had mounted free enterprise expeditions

to seize the territories of any native ruler too weak to resist them. What they gained at their own risk and expense, and held 'by the power of their swords and of fortune' against Welsh counter-attacks and rival Normans alike, they passed on to

Early fourteenth-century effigy of a de Barry knight, in Manorbier church (By courtesy of the National Monuments Record, Wales).

their descendants as 'Marcher lordships', private kingdoms in all but name. By the time of Gerald's birth, this fiercely independent warrior aristocracy occupied much of eastern Wales, and dominated all the south coast from Chepstow to St Davids. While he was still in his twenties, his own kinsmen would lead them across the western sea to the conquest of Ireland.

Though periodically threatened by the still formidable native rulers of the north and west — one of Gerald's earliest memories was of a Welsh raid on his homeland — the Marchers were not always on bad terms with their Welsh neighbours, and at times it suited them to secure or extend their conquests by marrying Welsh princesses. Thus Gerald of Windsor had married the beautiful Nest, daughter of the famous Rhys ap Tewdwr, and through this well-connected Welsh grandmother our Gerald inherited the blood of almost all the princely families in the land. Through her he likewise acquired an unusually large number of cousins and uncles — some Welsh, some part-Norman, some legitimate, and some otherwise. For, quite apart from Gerald's mother and the four other children she bore her husband, Nest also produced at least five more by a series of high-born lovers, including no less a person than King Henry I of England. Whether she conceived this

Gerald's grandmother, the beautiful Princess Nest — the 'Helen of Wales' — included King Henry I among her many lovers (By permission of the British Library, Additional Ms. 10292, f.21).

'Set on a rocky spur overlooking the Severn Sea' — Manorbier Castle, Gerald's birthplace. In the distance is the beach where he played as a boy.

unofficial brood before, after or during her marriage is unclear, but the last seems most likely. Certainly she was more than suspected of arranging her own abduction by a lovestruck Welsh prince — an incident which provoked her outraged husband (who had been forced to make an undignified escape from his own castle via a privy) to hunt down and eventually kill her abductor. Naturally enough, Gerald wrote little about his remarkable grandmother's romantic entanglements: yet he was proud to boast that, through her, 'he was related to all the great men of Wales, of either nation'.

Pride of birth, indeed, is a recurrent theme in Gerald's writings. He was proud of his Welsh royal blood; prouder still of being a Marcher — one of the select band of pioneers who 'inherit our courage from the Welsh, and our skill in warfare from the Normans'; and the proudest of all of belonging to the Norman-Welsh fitz Geralds — the 'sons of Gerald', as all the descendants of Nest were called, whether or not they were actually related to Gerald of Windsor. 'Who penetrate the enemy's strongholds?' he demanded, 'the fitz Geralds!; Who protect their native land? The fitz Geralds!; Who do the foemen fear? The fitz Geralds!': and then, more ominously, 'Who are assailed by envy? The fitz Geralds'.

Gerald himself was to find his mixed Norman-Welsh blood very much a mixed blessing. When the kings of England required a diplomat capable of negotiating both with Welsh princes and Norman barons, or when Archbishop Baldwin needed an informed guide through both Welsh and Marcher lands, Gerald was greatly in demand. But when it came to rewards or advancement — and particularly when Gerald strove to become bishop of St Davids — then the Normans could choose to reject him as a Welshman, and the Welsh dismiss him as a Norman interloper. 'Were Gerald not a Welshman', remarked King Henry II, 'he would

Cilgerran Castle above the River Teifi, perhaps the scene of Nest's abduction.

Gerald's half-Welsh, half-Norman uncle, Robert fitz Stephen. From a twelfth-century manuscript of Gerald's Conquest of Ireland — Expugnatio Hibernica (By courtesy of the National Library of Ireland, Ms. 700).

Manorbier church and castle from the north-west.

be worthy of high honour': and when a clerical rival wished to blacken his name, 'He denounced me to the Normans as a Welshman and an enemy, while to the Welsh he called me a Norman, and thus hostile to them on principle'.

As yet unaffected by these frustrations, Gerald's childhood was certainly a happy one. It was spent at his father's castle of Manorbier in southern Pembroke, set on a rocky spur overlooking the 'Severn Sea'. In later life he remembered its orchard and tall hazel-nut trees, its deep fishpond and its sweet sea air, and unashamedly proclaimed it the most delightful place in all Wales. He was the youngest of four brothers, who often played together — no doubt talking in Norman-French, the normal language of the Marchers and their cousins in England and France, and one which Gerald used for everyday speech all his life. Doubtless, too, Welsh was sometimes heard at Manorbier. Possibly Angharad taught it to her children, and Gerald clearly knew enough to speculate on the origins of Welsh words or compare the dialects of north and south Wales. Yet he probably never learnt to speak Welsh really fluently — at least, he never admits to that ability. His knowledge of English (a language then far closer to King Alfred's Anglo-Saxon than to its modern descendant) was sketchier still, and certainly he never spoke it willingly — indeed, he scornfully compared it to the hissing of geese, lambasting the English as 'the most worthless race under Heaven . . . In their own country they are the slaves of the Normans, and in Wales they serve only as cowherds . . . and cleaners of sewers'.

As soon as he could think for himself, young Gerald decided on a career as a churchman. Even on the beach, when his brothers — budding knights — built sand-castles and sand-palaces, he preferred sand-churches and sand-monasteries, and when Manorbier was roused by the alarm of a Welsh raid, the frightened boy begged to be carried to the

The early twelfth-century nave of St Peter's Abbey, now Gloucester Cathedral, which Gerald knew as a schoolboy.

outstripped all his contemporaries.

When he was thought old enough to leave home, probably at the age of nine or ten, Gerald was sent to continue his studies at the great Benedictine abbey of St Peter's at Gloucester, whose church survives as Gloucester Cathedral — the magnificent Norman pillars of its nave must have been a familiar sight to him. Schools attached to cathedrals and great monasteries were the only worthwhile educational establishments in twelfth-century Britain, and presumably Uncle David considered Gloucester's more suitable than any in Wales. There, under 'that most learned scholar, Master Haimon', Gerald will have learnt advanced Latin grammer, also beginning the study of logic and rhetoric — the ability to argue clearly and persuasively, which proved to be Gerald's speciality.

unfortified village church, preferring this spiritual refuge to the more conventional protection of the castle keep. Looking back, Gerald saw such events as back, Gerald saw such events as evidence of divine guidance. But to his father (who jokingly nicknamed him 'my bishop') his choice made very good sense, for as the youngest son Gerald had little chance of inheriting the family estates — besides, his uncle David fitz Gerald had recently become bishop of St Davids, and could help him considerably in his career.

Gloucester Cathedral from the south.

But the learning Gloucester could provide was limited, and by the time Gerald had reached his middle teens he was ready to move on to higher education. Since there were as yet no universities in Britain, the obvious choice was the great University of Paris, the most famous and attractive in Europe. Its courses were long, arduous and expensive, and the ten years or so Gerald spent there during his first visit alone (he was to return twice more) were nothing out of the ordinary for scholars who hoped for high office in the Church. Although he found time — foreshadowing both his later fascination with 'unnatural history' and his tendency to credulousness — to record the recapture of an escaped lion by the Parisian woman who made perverted love to it, he claims to have been a depressingly model student: 'so wholly devoted to his studies, and so free from levity and frivolity . . . that whenever the arts lecturers desired a pattern of excellence, with one accord they named Gerald'. No doubt, therefore, he felt ready to tackle anything when he returned to Wales in about 1174, and plunged straight into the controversies which were to occupy most of his long life.

To this uncle his education was entrusted, and the first step was to teach him Latin, the language of the Universal Church and of every learned man in Christendom. In future, Gerald would use it to converse easily with clerics from Ireland to Rome, and his seventeen surviving books — all written in excellent Latin — prove him the greatest master of the language Wales has ever produced. Yet he made a slow start, distracted by his brothers' excited chatter of wars and tournaments. Not until his teachers stung him with insults — 'thick, thicker, thickest!' they chanted, 'silly, sillier, silliest!' — did he make any progress, but then (as he himself modestly tells us) he soon far

Many medieval university scholars continued their education into their twenties or thirties. This fourteenth-century illustration shows scholars at work, from a medical treatise (By permission of the British Library, Harleian Ms. 3745, f.1).

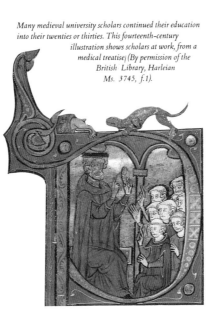

The Twelfth-Century Church in Wales

by Glanmor Williams

In the twelfth century the Church dominated not only the religion but also much of the public life, politics, and culture of Wales, as of other European countries. Its bishops and abbots were among the rulers' wealthiest and most influential tenants-in-chief; a crucial source of potential support in men and money. Leading clerics were much the best-educated men of the age and indispensable to princes as advisers and administrators. The Church, too, was the focus of profound regional and national loyalties, with its shrines as the external symbols of God's covenant with his people. It ultimately sanctioned the exercise of all religious and secular authority; and, most significant of all, controlled the means of salvation in the world to come — a world intensely real to most men and women.

In Wales the territorial boundaries of diocese, archdeaconry, rural deanery, and parish were being fixed for the first time, and regular payment of tithe

A page from Rhigyfarch's Psalter, written at Llanbadarn Fawr about 1079 (see p. 57). The scholar-cleric, Rhigyfarch, is perhaps better known for his life of St David written about 1085-95 (By permission of the Board of Trinity College, Dublin, Ms. 50).

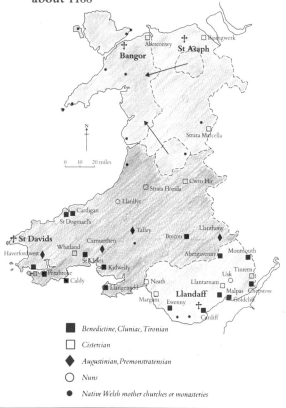

The Dioceses and Monasteries of Wales, about 1188

- Aberconwy
- St Asaph
- Basingwerk
- Bangor
- Strata Marcella
- 0 10 20 miles
- Cwm Hir
- Strata Florida
- Llanllyr
- Cardigan
- St Dogmael's
- Talley
- Brecon
- Llanthony
- St Davids
- Whitland
- Carmarthen
- Abergavenny
- Monmouth
- Haverfordwest
- St Kears
- Kidwelly
- Usk
- Tintern
- Pembroke
- Caldy
- Llangenydd
- Neath
- Llantarnam
- Malpas
- Chepstow
- Margam
- Ewenny
- Llandaff
- Goldcliff
- Cardiff

- ■ Benedictine, Cluniac, Tironian
- □ Cistercian
- ◆ Augustinian, Premonstratensian
- ○ Nuns
- ● Native Welsh mother churches or monasteries

introduced. A constant round of worship and supplication in Latin was maintained in all cathedrals and monasteries, and on a lesser scale in parish churches. On Sundays and holy days, and in monasteries every day, mass was offered. The Church appropriately commemorated Christmas, Easter, Whitsun, and other festivals of the Christian calendar and presided at all the great milestones of human existence: birth, marriage, and death. It encouraged pilgrims to visit holy places, where they venerated saints and their relics, and sought health and succour for themselves, their animals and crops. Public health, charitable giving, solemnizing of agreements, and disposal of property after death were the preserve of the Church. So was most of such education as was available; and at the ecclesiastical scriptoria scribes painstakingly copied and preserved manuscripts and stored them. Spearheaded by the vigorous and reforming papacy of the age, the Church and its clerics were confident of their own elevated and sacred mission and eager to assert it.

Such all-pervading influence made it vital for lay rulers to enlist or coerce the aid of the churchmen in all their major acts of policy. In Wales, since the end of the eleventh century, the Church had been extensively used by Norman kings, barons, and archbishops of Canterbury to overcome native resistance. Bishops of Welsh dioceses had been compelled to acknowledge Canterbury's overlordship. Continental-type monasteries of the Benedictine and Augustinian orders had been introduced into newly-established Norman boroughs and endowed with possessions formerly belonging to the Welsh Church.

The Benedictine priory at Ewenny, in the southern March, was established in 1141 by the Norman lord, Maurice de Londres (see p. 40). The nave still serves as a parish church (Photograph by David Robinson).

A page from the Black Book of Carmarthen, probably written at the Augustinian priory of St John's, Carmarthen, between 1170 and 1230. It contains 'popular' religious verse, and is a rare survival of this early period (By courtesy of the National Library of Wales, Peniarth Ms. 1, f.18).

The Carew Cross, Dyfed, is thought to commemorate Maredudd ap Edwin who died in battle in 1035. Such distinctive crosses often point to the existence of a major pre-Conquest church nearby (Photograph by Roger Vlitos).

Any attempts by Welsh clerics to claim autonomy for themselves had been snuffed out by Normans in Church and State.

These policies had not gone unresisted. Welsh princes tried to prevent Welsh bishops from bowing the knee to Canterbury. They handsomely endowed Cistercian monasteries like Strata Florida or Aberconwy, whose holy life, strict discipline, pastoral farming, attention to education, and patronage of literature and patriotic sentiment won them a unique place in Welsh affections. They also supported the efforts of clerics to promote the rights of St Davids as an independent province.

Strikingly representative of most of the trends mentioned above was Giraldus Cambrensis. He was acutely conscious of the reforming tendencies of the twelfth century and deeply aware of the need to extend and intensify their influence in Wales. This made him an ardent champion of the papacy and its leadership of church improvement and the crusading movement. Descended, as he himself said, 'from the princes of Wales and the [Norman] barons of the March', he nevertheless 'hated injustice in whichever nation he saw it'. He therefore argued with more substance, vigour, and ingenuity than anyone else for the rights of the Welsh and especially of his beloved St Davids. His fluent pen, percipient eye, and colourful personality make him one of the liveliest and appealing men of the age.

Originally founded in 1164, the Cistercian abbey of Strata Florida soon attracted the enthusiastic support and patronage of the Lord Rhys. Unlike many monastic foundations in the March, this house was to win a distinct place in the affections of the Welsh princes (Photograph by David Robinson).

Gerald the Archdeacon

The Gerald who returned to Wales in his late twenties was a striking figure — tall, good-looking ('remarkable for beauty of face and form' he admits with his usual candour) and made still more formidable by his huge bushy eyebrows. With his powerful family connections as well as his distinguished degree from the best university in Europe, he was clearly destined for great things, and the benefices he was immediately given — he became rector of several parishes in Wales and England — were only a beginning. He was not, of

The church of Mathry, Dyfed, was among those granted to Gerald (Photograph by Roger Vlitos).

course, expected to act as a mere parish priest in any of these places. According to the usual custom of the day, they would be served by humble curates while Gerald employed their income to support his greater mission.

That mission, only too obvious to a cleric imbued with the latest ideas from Paris, was nothing less than the reform of the Church in Wales — a notoriously lax and old-fashioned institution, whose supposedly celibate priests openly kept 'wives' and whose right and incomes were everywhere usurped by bullying knights and princes. Gerald's own family were by no means shining examples of righteousness (his uncle, Bishop David, habitually sold off church lands to maintain his brood of illegitimate children) while he

himself frequently called on the armed support of his relatives in ecclesiastical disputes. But such inconsistencies did nothing to blunt his reforming zeal, and the first to experience it were those inhabitants of Pembrokeshire who refused to hand over the 'tithes' (or tenths) of their wool and cheese due to the Church. Armed with a special mandate from the archbishop of Canterbury himself, and deterred neither by foul weather nor threats against his life, Gerald rode about the region bringing them to heel. When the powerful sheriff of Pembroke defied him, Gerald immediately excommunicated him with bell, book and candle, forcing him to submit to a painful beating before the dreaded sentence was lifted.

Next, in about 1175, he turned his attention to Brecon, whose aged archdeacon he discovered living comfortably with a mistress — whereupon Gerald turned him out of office and (with the help of Uncle David) became archdeacon of Brecon himself. This post brought him both an official residence at Llanddew — a pleasant house, he reported 'which I would not change for all the riches of Croesus' — and the welcome duty of reforming the local clergy's morals. Accustomed to the happy-go-lucky rule of his predecessor, the clergy were not so enthusiastic about being reformed. Indeed, when Gerald embarked on an official 'visitation' of remote Rhwng Gwy a Hafren (now the Radnorshire district of Powys) they did all they could to frustrate

Gerald's archdiaconal church at Llanddew, Powys, seen beyond a doorway of the bishop's palace.

him, first by threats and rumours, then by showering his servants with arrows, and finally by besieging him in the church of Llanbadarn Fawr, near Llandrindod Wells. The archdeacon, however, now brought his extensive network of relationships into play, sending a plea for help to his cousin Cadwallon ap Madog, the local ruler: at the news of Cadwallon's vengeful approach, the besiegers had no alternative but abject surrender.

No sooner had the archdeacon returned home to Llanddew than another crisis blew up. Bishop Adam of St Asaph was reported on his way to consecrate the new church at Kerry near Newtown, in a district which rightfully belonged to Gerald's own diocese of St Davids: if he succeeded, St Davids might suffer a

The early-Norman entrance arch of Llanbadarn Fawr church, Powys, where Gerald was besieged.

serious loss of territory. Gathering armed support as he went, Gerald therefore hastened northwards at once, just managing to occupy the disputed church before the bishop arrived. A richly comic episode followed, with bishop and archdeacon matching claim and counter-claim at the churchyard gate, and eventually threatening to excommunicate each other. Donning his mitre for greater effect, Bishop Adam actually began to shout out his

A bishop consecrates a church, from Bishop Anian of Bangor's Pontifical, about 1320-28 (By courtesy of the Dean and Chapter of Bangor Cathedral).

solemn curse, but Gerald shouted his own still louder, reinforcing it by signalling his men to sound the much-feared excommunication toll on the church bells. This was too much for the bishop. He faltered, panicked, and then galloped off at full tilt, pursued by a volley of

Kerry church, Powys, the scene of Gerald's triumph over Bishop Adam of St Asaph.

stones from Gerald's jeering supporters. Gerald later completed his triumph by recounting it to King Henry II, who roared with laughter at the tale.

Though he continued as archdeacon for twenty-eight years (1175-1203), Gerald's more pressing concerns increasingly prevented him

from pursuing his duties with such single-minded vigour. Yet he never abandoned his ideal of reforming the Welsh country clergy, and in about 1197 he wrote for them a lively instruction manual entitled *Gemma Ecclesiastica* — *The Jewel of the Church*. In it he warns them against everyday malpractices like substituting cider for communion wine, allowing all-night popular song sessions in the churchyard — next morning, a bemused priest had sung out 'Sweetheart, help me', instead of 'The Lord be with you' — and making simple mistakes in their Latin: one parson promised his bishop two hundred sheep (*oves*) when he meant to say eggs (*ova*), and was then forced to produce the sheep. His sternest prohibitions, however, were against living with women, a practice not only sinful but also inconvenient (they filled the parsonage with midwives, cradles and howling infants) and expensive (they demanded new dresses for market-going and even commandeered the vicarage horse, making the parson walk behind). Much better, counsels Gerald, never to look at women at all, let alone sit drinking with them at

Mixing with women, Gerald warned his clergy, could only result in trouble. An erring priest and lady in the stocks, from a fourteenth-century manuscript (By permission of the British Library, Royal Ms. 10 E IV, f. 187).

Two pages from the only surviving copy of Gerald's manual for the clergy, The Jewel of the Church — Gemma Ecclesiastica *(By courtesy of His Grace the Archbishop of Canterbury and the Trustees of Lambeth Palace Library, Lambeth Palace Ms. 236, ff. 4v-5).*

parish festivals. All this good advice is backed up with learned quotations, the latest theological notions and (Gerald being Gerald) with tales of flying crucifixes, lustful demons,

greedy bishops, and hard-swearing monarchs. Of the last he spoke from personal experience, for in his middle years Gerald the archdeacon became Gerald the Plantagenet courtier.

'Following the Court'
Gerald the Royal Servant and his Visit to Ireland

'**A**s Gerald's fame increased and became more widely known, King Henry II summoned him to his presence . . . and although he was most unwilling . . . he became a follower of the court'. Thus, in July 1184, Gerald began his ten years in the service of the Plantagenet kings — perhaps not quite so reluctantly as he pretended, since he knew well that a period at court often led to the high church offices he so much desired. Admittedly it had its drawbacks, for following the court meant following the king, and Henry II was probably the most energetic monarch in history. His dominions stretched from the Pyrenees to the Scottish border, and he ceaselessly travelled about them at breakneck speed, hotly pursued by a large and usually exasperated household. Even after a hard day's hunting, reported Gerald, he rarely sat down (so that his retainers also had to stand all evening) and he took a positive delight in

The red-haired, irascible King Henry II, uncharacteristically shown seated in this twelfth-century manuscript of Gerald's Conquest of Ireland — Expugnatio Hibernica *(By courtesy of the National Library of Ireland, Ms. 700).*

sudden changes of plan, often halting unexpectedly in places so remote that his courtiers had nowhere to sleep. According to Walter Map, Gerald's fellow-courtier and fellow-Marcher, Henry's exertions stemmed from his terror of growing fat. In his service, Map complained, 'We wear out our clothes, our bodies and our horses . . . in vain and entirely unfruitful haste we are borne on our insane course. Truly the court is a place of punishment, and only milder than Hell in that those it torments can at least escape by dying'.

The Plantagenet Court was almost continuously on the road. This early fourteenth-century illustration from the Luttrell Psalter shows royal ladies in a travelling carriage, followed by mounted courtiers (By permission of the British Library, Additional Ms. 42130, f.181).

Henry II's great keep at Dover Castle, Kent. It was the king's most ambitious and extravagant castle-building work (By courtesy of English Heritage).

horrified Henry II, who first cut off Marcher reinforcements and then went in person to enforce his authority. Neither expedient worked, so in 1185 the king decided to declare his nineteen year old son John 'lord of Ireland', and sent him over to solve the problem once and for all. With him went Gerald, whose influence over his kinsmen among the invaders was thought likely to smooth the young prince's progress.

The mission was a catastrophic failure from the very moment John set foot on shore, to be greeted by a deputation of loyal but exceedingly hairy Irish chieftains. Hooting with derision, the prince's modishly clean-shaven young friends began to pull them about by their long beards,

sending them off in a high dudgeon to sharpen their axes for war. John then proceeded to outrage both Marchers and Irish allies by transferring their estates to his raw hangers-on, who scorned the advice of the battle-hardened settlers and went blundering into bogs in their heavy armour. Nor can Gerald have improved matters by attacking the ancient customs of the Irish Church, which he mocked for not yet producing a martyr — 'Now that you Normans have arrived', retorted an Irish cleric, 'it very soon will'. After a few months, therefore, John slunk home in disgrace, but Gerald remained longer, and for him at least the expedition proved momentous. Having discovered a talent for authorship, he was writing two books about Ireland.

Luckily for Gerald, he was frequently detached from this travelling madhouse on diplomatic missions to his relations among the Welsh princes. His principal value to the Crown, indeed, was his ability to negotiate easily with his first cousin, Rhys ap Gruffudd of Deheubarth, much the most powerful Welsh ruler — at Hereford in 1184 he even dared to tease Rhys publicly about the rivalry between their respective families, and later he helped to calm the old prince's fury at being insulted by King Richard I. His usefulness, however, was not confined to Wales, for some of his closer kinsmen were causing the Plantagenets a great deal of trouble elsewhere.

In 1167, while Gerald was still at university, his uncle Robert fitz Stephen (one of grandmother Nest's illegitimate brood) had led a force of Marcher knights to Ireland at the request of the disreputable King Dermot MacMurrough. Unleashed against Dermot's Irish rivals, these ninety mailed Norman riders and their three hundred expert Welsh archers had a shattering effect. More and more Marchers crossed from Wales to join them, and before long they seemed likely to conquer all Ireland, turning it into a Norman-Welsh empire quite independent of the English Crown. This prospect

Gerald's princely companion in Ireland, later King John, lies beneath this splendid tomb in Worcester Cathedral (By courtesy of the National Monuments Record, England).

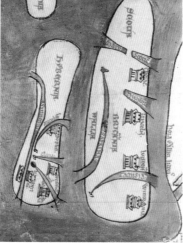

A ferociously simplified map of Britain and Ireland, showing the latter enlarged out of scale, with Iceland just to the north. From a twelfth-century manuscript of Gerald's Topography of Ireland — Topographia Hibernica *(By courtesy of the National Library of Ireland, Ms. 700).*

One of these, the *Conquest of Ireland (Expugnatio Hibernica),* is a chronicle of the Marcher invasion from the heavily biased viewpoint of Gerald's kinsmen, and a vivid picture gallery of fitz Gerald heroes. Brother

Robert, gallantly storming Wexford, is struck down by a stone (sixteen years later his teeth fell out as a result, but miraculously grew back again); cousin Meiler fitz Henry hacks his way through an Irish ambush, 'lopping off a hand here, an arm there, and elsewhere a whole head and shoulders'; while uncle Robert fitz Stephen, despite his 'excessive addiction to wine and women', routs vast numbers of enemies with his tiny band of Normans and Welshmen.

Gerald's *Topography of Ireland (Topographia Hibernica)* is far more remarkable. For this first and most widely-read of all his major works (it was even translated into the Provençal language of southern France) sets out to do something no-one had attempted since Roman times: to describe the history, geography, wildlife and customs of a land and its people. The result is an extraordinary blend of acute observation, wild guesswork and very tall stories — some of them probably passed on by Irishmen delighted to mislead a gullible tourist. Gerald describes the habits of ospreys and dippers with a reasonable accuracy, but declared that barnacle geese are hatched from barnacle shells: he understood why Ireland is so wet, but believed that Irish shoelaces dispel poison. The Irish saints, he discovered, were an exceptionally touchy and vindictive crew, regularly bursting, incinerating or transforming into werewolves those that crossed them. The kindly St Kevin, conversely, allowed a blackbird to nest in his hand, never moving until her chicks grew up. As for the Irish people, pronounced Gerald the violently prejudiced Marcher, they were handsome, tough, and wonderful musicians. But they were also disgustingly barbarous, treacherous, bad-tempered and violent, ever ready to lash out with the deadly axes they carried instead of civilized Norman swords or Welsh longbows.

In Ireland, therefore, the *Topography* remains controversial to

this day, and even in Gerald's time many thought it impossibly far-fetched. But its author was immensely proud of his pioneering book, and devised a novel (if

The wonders of Ireland — Barnacle geese hatching from barnacle shells, from a thirteenth-century 'bestiary' (By permission of the British Library, Harleian Ms. 4751, f.36).

A fatal quarrel between bad-tempered Irish axemen, from a manuscript of Gerald's Topography of Ireland — Topographia Hibernica, *about 1200 (By permission of the British Library, Royal Ms. 13 B VIII, f.28).*

expensive) method of publicizing it: he publicly read it aloud at Oxford over a period of three days, guaranteeing himself listeners by feeding all the local poor on the first day, the clergy and scholars on the second, and the gentry and citizens on the third. There is no doubt that he also expected far more distinguished and influential readers, for his *Topography* is dedicated in the most flattering terms to King Henry II, and his *Conquest* to the future King Richard I.

Neither these literary offerings nor his faithful service as courtier and diplomat, however, won Gerald the royal favour he hoped for. When he retired in disgust from the court in about 1194, he had gained nothing from the Plantagenets but 'empty promises void of all truth'. The obstacles to his advancement, he now realized, were the very qualities that had made him so useful to the Crown — his birth in Wales and his kinship with the Welsh princes. Before long, these same factors would contribute to a still more bitter disappointment, indeed the greatest of Gerald's life.

St Kevin, an unusually patient Irish saint, holding the blackbird which nested in his hand. He sits on an animal-headed throne (By permission of the British Library, Royal Ms. 13 B VIII, f.20).

Gerald and The Kings of the English

by Ralph A. Griffiths

Gerald's character sketches of the three kings who ruled England during most of his life — Henry II (1154–89), Richard I (1189–99), and John (1199–1216) — are among the most vivid and oft-quoted descriptions of medieval kings. They are acute and witty, often salacious, sometimes malicious, and they are illustrated by stories, including some set in Wales. His picture of King Henry in his fifties rings true:

> [He] had hair that was almost red in colour, grey eyes and a large round head. His eyes were bright, and in anger fierce and flecked with red. He had a fiery complexion, his voice was husky, his neck bent forward a little from his shoulders, and he had a broad chest and powerful arms. His body was fleshy, and he had a very large belly, naturally so, and not due to the effects of gluttony . . . In order that he might keep this defect of nature under control and mitigate its effects, and improve the shortcomings of his body by the sterling quality of his mind, . . . he used to torment his body with an excessive amount of exercise. (*The Conquest of Ireland, 1188*)

Gerald's wit and malice were directed — after the king's death — at Henry's mistress, Rosamund Clifford:

> Until then [1173] the king had kept his adultery secret, but it later became common knowledge, for, from her being Fair Rosamund in the everyday and indeed quite unwarranted sense of the word [*rosa mundi*], he was really debasing her into what she came to be called quite openly and shamelessly, that tart Rosie [*rosa immundi*]. (*On the Instruction of a Prince, 1217–8*)

Others had as good an opportunity as Gerald to observe the kings at close quarters; but none had Gerald's advantages when it came to recording memorable personal impressions of them. It was Gerald's rare talent to see the Angevins in the round, as rulers of a vast 'empire', most of whose lands he knew. He had been a student in Paris for many years and moved as easily in France as he did in England, whilst his upbringing in south Wales and his family interests in Ireland provided a unique vantage point from which to judge the kings. And as one of the luminaries of the twelfth-century Renaissance, he could compose imperishable portraits that have powerfully affected our view of all three of them.

Gerald's family was well known at court: Henry II was the grandson of Henry I, whilst Gerald was the grandson of Henry I's mistress, the beautiful Nest.

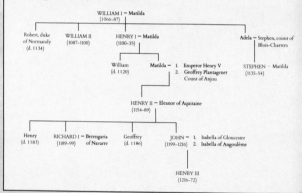

A simplified Genealogical Table showing the descent of the Kings of the English during Gerald's lifetime

The tomb effigy of Eleanor of Aquitaine at Fontevrault Abbey, Poitou, France. Gerald was to consider her marriage to Henry II (only a few weeks after her match with Louis VII of France had been nullified) a scandalous affair (Photograph by Giraudon, Paris).

Depictions of four kings of England, from the Historia Anglorum (1250–9) by Matthew Paris, chronicler of St Albans Abbey. The panel shows: top left, Henry II; top right, Richard I; bottom left, John; bottom right, Henry III (By permission of the British Library, Royal Ms. 14 C VII, f.9).

The gateway at Newcastle, Bridgend, where the details suggest a rebuilding about 1183–89. This exceptional work may have been undertaken by Henry II since he held the castle in ward at this time. Elsewhere, the king was engaged in major castle-building, including the great keep at Dover (see p. 16).

'. . . hair that was almost red in colour, grey eyes and a large round head'. So runs Gerald's description of Henry II in his fifties. The king was buried in Fontevrault Abbey church, where this splendid effigy now lies (Photograph by Giraudon, Paris).

They may have met in 1176, when Henry II rejected Gerald as bishop of St Davids. Most likely it was Gerald's knowledge of Ireland, gained in 1183 when he visited relatives who had settled there, and of his native Wales that caused Henry to summon him to court (1184). He spent the next ten years in the service of Henry and Richard I, and knew them both well. Henry seemed courageous and compassionate, approachable and generous, diligent and yet short-tempered, and addicted to hunting in all weather. Gerald's description of Richard is famous and set the tone of the king's subsequent reputation:

> . . . he cared for no success that was not reached by a path cut by his own sword and stained with the blood of his adversaries . . . our lion-hearted prince, who is more than a lion . . . (*The Topography of Ireland*, 1188)

Richard I seems to have become a popular hero within a short time of his death in 1199. One of the legends which grew up around him was his meeting in single combat with Saladin. These fourteenth-century tiles from Neath Abbey show the king with a shield and lance, and Saladin with a round buckler and scimitar (By permission of the National Museum of Wales).

Gerald's Irish experience was put to good use in 1185 when he accompanied Henry's youngest son, John, to Ireland: he sailed from Milford Haven in John's ship and spent some time with the eighteen-year-old prince. Gerald formed a not unfavourable impression of him, but after living through John's reign he came to dislike the king vehemently: 'a tyrannous whelp, who issued from the most bloody tyrants and was the most tyrannous of them all'. (*On the Instruction of a Prince*, 1217-8)

A fourteenth-century manuscript illustration depicting King John hunting (By permission of the British Library, Cotton Claudius, D II, f.116).

To judge by Gerald's journeys to France with Henry II (1189) and to troubled Wales, his abilities were highly prized by Henry and Richard. He had less opportunity to get to know Henry II's eldest sons — Young Henry died in 1183, Geoffrey in 1186 — but that did not stop him from making trenchant remarks about them, especially about the silver-tongued Geoffrey:

> . . . overflowing with words, smooth as oil, possessed, by his syrupy and persuasive eloquence, of the power of dissolving the apparently indissoluble, able to corrupt two kingdoms with his tongue . . .

Built largely during 1196-98, Richard I's great castle of Château Gaillard, on the borders of Normandy, was novel in its concentric construction and dominated the Seine valley (Photograph by Peter Humphries).

His hankering after St Davids kept Gerald's interest in the court and its intrigues alive under Richard and John, even though he retired to Lincoln in 1194 to live the life of a secluded scholar.

Not that Gerald's opinions are completely reliable: they tell us as much about Gerald as they do about Henry, Richard and John. During thirty years of writing, he changed his mind about people: certainly he claimed that he was afraid to write plainly about Henry II during the king's lifetime; and in dedicating *The Topography of Ireland* to Henry II ('our western Alexander') and *The Conquest of Ireland* first to Richard and then to John, he showed himself anxious for their favour. A cleric's outrage may partly explain Gerald's growing criticism of Henry and John for paying scant regard to the Church and neglecting their devotions. Above all, the ebb and flow of his own fortunes gradually distorted Gerald's vision. His failure to secure St Davids made him bitter towards the kings, even venomous in gossiping about them. By the time he finished *On the Instruction of a Prince* (1217-8), he was deeply hostile to them all. The rebellions of Henry II's sons and the disasters of Henry's last years he now regarded as God's judgement on the king's waywardness in marrying the French king's former wife, Eleanor of Aquitaine, and oppressing the

A page from the fourteenth-century surviving manuscript of On the Instruction of a Prince. In it, Gerald is bitterly hostile to the Plantagenet dynasty (By permission of the British Library, Cotton Julius B XIII, f.48).

Church: a tyrant and deservedly fallen. Gerald's final portrait of Henry is a caricature of certain character defects which he had observed thirty years before:

> From beginning to end an oppressor of the nobility; weighing right and wrong, what is lawful and unlawful, by his own interest; a seller and delayer of justice; shifty in speech and full of craft; readily breaking, not his word only, but his pledged honour and his oath; an open adulterer; ungrateful towards God and without devotion; a hammer of the Church, and born to destruction.

Gerald also believed in Fate and prophecies: he became convinced that the Wheel of Fortune had begun its downward turn following the murder of Thomas Becket (1170) by Henry's knights. Gerald's earthly loyalties changed too. Of Anglo-Norman stock, born in Wales and living mostly in England, his mind was a jumble of sympathies. His Anglo-French loyalties were gradually submerged by Welsh ones, especially when it appeared that his Welsh (and Irish) connections told against him as a candidate for St Davids. *On the Instruction of a Prince* reveals a grotesquely partisan Gerald who even preferred the Capetian kings of France to the Angevins he had long served. He repeated the legend of 'an accursed race' sprung from a demon-countess and further tainted by the immoralities of Henry II's father and mother, and Henry's own scandalous liaison with Eleanor of Aquitaine. He reported Richard I's own words: 'What wonder if we lack the natural affections of mankind — we came from the Devil, and must needs go back to the Devil'. The Angevins' habit of swearing by God's eyes, teeth, feet, throat and death was symbolically blasphemous; so was their use of bears, leopards and lions as badges compared with the lilies preferred by French kings.

Compelling Gerald's portraits of Henry, Richard and John may be, but they were dynamic constructions that offer a challenge to their would-be interpreter.

The tomb effigy of King Richard I, in the abbey church at Fontevrault, Poitou, France (Photograph by Giraudon, Paris).

'This Man's Noble Deed'
Gerald and the Struggle for St Davids

Bishop Anselm le Gros of St Davids (1230-45), an Englishman, from his tomb in the cathedral (By courtesy of the National Monuments Record, Wales).

*A*s though foreshadowing the many trials to come, Gerald's struggle to become bishop of St Davids got off to a very bad start indeed. In 1176, when he was still a young archdeacon, the local clergy nominated him as a candidate to succeed his uncle David in the post. He was nominated, not elected, for no bishop might be appointed without the prior permission of the king of England and the archbishop of Canterbury. Yet a mere rumour that he had been chosen sent Henry II into one of his notorious Plantagenet rages, and even when the misunderstanding was cleared up he utterly refused to consider Gerald as a candidate. A man like Gerald, related to the Welsh princes and a vigorous champion of the rights of St Davids, was the very last bishop Henry wanted for the most controversial diocese in Wales.

The controversy over St Davids sprang from the tradition that its founder, St David himself, had been archbishop of all Wales. Both he and his successors, moreover, were believed to have been 'metropolitan' archbishops — which is to say, the heads of an independent Welsh Church, owing no allegiance whatever to the English archbishops of Canterbury. At some time in the past, the story ran, their *pallium* or archbishops' vestment of office had been taken to Brittany, and never returned. Yet they had retained their special position until the invading Normans had forcibly and illegally subjugated the Welsh clergy to English domination, reducing St Davids to the status of an ordinary bishopric. If right were done, however, the archbishops of St Davids would once again rule a free Welsh Church.

The lavishly-decorated late-Norman arches of St Davids Cathedral nave were built during the time of Gerald's rival, Bishop Peter de Leia (1176-98).

Historically, this claim rested on extremely shaky ground, but its implications were enormous — especially if the Pope could be persuaded to support it. For if the highest authority in Christendom liberated the Welsh Church from the rule of English archbishops, might not the next step be the liberation of all Wales from the rule of English kings? Alarmed by this spectre, the English authorities resolved to keep a tight rein on the bishops of St Davids, forcing them to swear never to raise the claim and always preferring candidates with few Welsh connections. Thus, in 1176, the Anglo-Norman Peter of Lee (Peter de Leia) became bishop in Gerald's place, and despite Gerald's efforts he swore the oath required.

St Davids Cathedral, with the splendid late-medieval bishop's palace in the foreground (Photograph by Roger Vlitos).

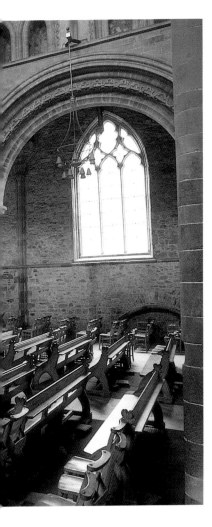

It was twenty-two years before the bishopric fell vacant again, and during that interval Gerald's interest in St Davids and its rights sometimes wavered. By accompanying Archbishop Baldwin of Canterbury on his official tour of Wales in 1188, for instance, he symbolically gave consent to English authority over the Welsh Church: while as a hopeful courtier he rejected two Welsh bishoprics (Llandaff and Bangor) 'because of the poverty of the land and the wickedness of the people'. What he wanted, he admitted, was a rich and peaceful English diocese, not a poor and controversial Welsh one. But the English bishopric never materialized, and the death of Bishop Peter in 1198 found Gerald an ageing and disappointed man. At the prospect of a fresh struggle for St Davids, however, his hopes revived, even though he knew the difficulties he must face. 'Would that the bishopric had never existed', he wrote, 'or rather that I had never been born in Wales, to suffer the slanders of my rivals'.

His most implacable opponent was Archbishop Hubert Walter, whom Gerald had bitterly offended and who returned his dislike with interest, swearing that neither he nor any other Welshman would ever be a bishop in Wales. But Hubert's opposition could perhaps be circumvented by appealing directly to the king, and here there was more hope, since Gerald's former master, Prince John, had recently come to the throne. Soon after his coronation, indeed, John apparently gave permission for the appointment — though he never made the decision public, and afterwards changed his mind — and on 22 June 1199 Gerald was unanimously elected bishop of St Davids. At this moment of apparent triumph, he 'delivered himself up without hesitation to the task of re-establishing the former state of his Church, and with it the honour of his country'. In other words, he was determined to become archbishop of all Wales, and to defend the Welsh Church and people against all comers: henceforward he would no longer be Gerald the Marcher or Gerald the courtier, but Gerald the Welsh patriot.

Formally, however, he was not yet Gerald the bishop. For all bishops must be ceremonially consecrated by their superiors, and independent St Davids could admit no superior in Britain: besides, the furious Hubert Walter was soon threatening to consecrate a rival English candidate of his own. Yet Hubert himself had a superior, the Pope, and if Gerald could gain papal consecration and papal support, the battle would be won. So to distant Rome he went, not once but three times during the next four years, braving bandits, warring armies, snowy Alpine passes and Hubert Walter's pursuing agents.

At first things seemed to be going well, and Gerald clearly hit it off with Innocent III, one of the greatest and most powerful popes of the Middle Ages. Innocent was delighted by a gift of Gerald's books (especially the *Jewel of the Church* which he kept by his bedside) and always gave him more than a fair chance to counter Hubert Walter's stream of anti-St Davids propaganda. According to his own account, indeed, Gerald made mincemeat of Hubert's arguments. Was Gerald unfitted for the bishopric by his Welsh birth? — then surely there should likewise be no English-born bishops in England: were the Welsh so barbarous that they needed the restraining hand of Canterbury? — then why did Hubert send only the dregs of the English clergy to rule them? As for Hubert himself, revealed Gerald, he was a fornicater, an arsonist, and very probably a heretic and a murderer; what was more, his Latin grammar was appalling.

While Gerald was scoring verbal points in Rome, however, his enemies were gaining ground in Wales. King John withdrew his support, and Hubert Walter's agents were progressively turning the St Davids clergy against him by a combination of blandishments, bribes (including counterfeit gold rings), and ever direr threats. His money was running out, and the faithless monks of Strata Florida cheated him of his precious

The supreme ruler of the Church — A pope and his cardinals in conclave, from a fourteenth-century manuscript (By permission of the British Library, Additional Ms. 23923, f.2).

books. The only consolation was that the princes of Wales — not only his kinsmen in Dyfed, but also Gwenwynwyn of Powys and the great Llywelyn of Gwynedd — now declared their firm and unanimous backing for his cause. Yet even this

The manuscript of Gerald's Jewel of the Church — Gemma Ecclesiastica — is stained by sea-water, perhaps a souvenir of its trip to Rome and back (By courtesy of His Grace the Archbishop of Canterbury and the Trustees of Lambeth Palace Library, Lambeth Palace Ms. 236, ff.67v–68).

proved double-edged, for it gave the English government the excuse to proclaim him a Welsh traitor and rebel, and on his second return from Rome Gerald found himself a hunted man, shunned by family and friends and denied lodging even in St Davids.

Entirely undaunted by his persecution, he resolved to appeal to Innocent once more, slipping across the Channel concealed in the bilges of a galley. But in Rome only disappointment awaited him: much though the Pope admired Gerald's persistence, he could not offend England by supporting him, and his election was annulled pending further investigation. Still he did not despair, even when he was imprisoned by a French robber knight while returning home. One of Hubert's agents had betrayed him,

identifying him by his shaggy eyebrows, but when his captors discovered that he had only twopence in his purse, they released Gerald and imprisoned the agent instead.

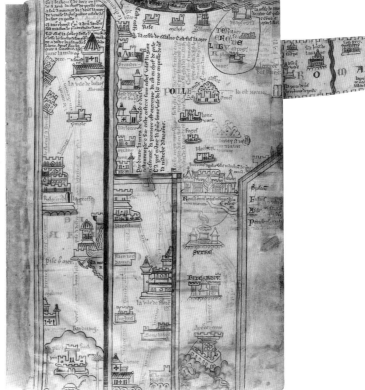

The last stages of the long road to Rome (shown top right) from a thirteenth-century liner map by Matthew Paris (By permission of the British Library, Royal Ms. 14 C VII, f.4).

Gerald is now honoured in St Davids Cathedral by this statue set up during the restoration of the Holy Trinity Chapel by A. D. Caroe in the 1920s.

By now, more than four years had passed since Gerald's election, and he was nearing sixty: his protests had lost none of their passion, but he was at last growing weary. The end came quite suddenly. On 10 November 1203, when Hubert Walter's nominee, Geoffrey of Henlawe, was elected bishop of St Davids, Gerald unexpectedly gave his consent. 'I have struggled enough', he announced to a thunderstruck audience, 'I have toiled sufficiently, and not without advantage . . . for I have revived the claim of our Church, which lay buried so long'. A few weeks later, moreover, he swore never to raise the issue again, and during the remaining twenty years of his life he never did so.

Gerald had failed, but he had failed only in the face of overwhelming odds, and he was honoured for it. 'As long as Wales shall last', pronounced Llywelyn the Great of Gwynedd, 'this man's noble deed shall be praised by poets and chroniclers. For he who does all he can and leaves nothing undone has deserved worthy praise, though perchance he fails in his desire'. Even now, Gerald's fight to free the Welsh Church from English domination is not forgotten, though another of his achievements is better remembered still: his famous Journey through Wales, and the delightful book he wrote about it.

Preaching the Cross

As this thirteenth-century 'map' shows, medieval Christians regarded Jerusalem as both literally and figuratively the centre of their world. Its capture by Saladin was therefore a shattering disaster (By permission of the British Library, Additional Ms. 28681, f.9).

During the late summer of 1187, astounding and terrible tidings spread through western Europe. The great Moslem warrior, Salah-ad-Din Yusuf, the dreaded 'Saladin', had surrounded the Christian army of Palestine at the Horns of Hattin, and utterly annhilated it: the Holy Cross of Christ, the sacred relic borne before the crusaders, was in the hands of the infidel. Within three months even worse news followed. Sweeping all before him, Saladin had taken the Holy City of Jerusalem, and

Jerusalem – Taken by Saladin in 1187, the mission to Wales by Gerald and Baldwin in 1188 was to raise support for a new crusade to free the Holy City from the infidel (Photograph by David Robinson).

only the desperately defended fortress of Tyre now held out against the final Moslem conquest of the land where Christ had lived and died.

Appalled by the magnitude of the disaster, Christendom reacted swiftly. All men, proclaimed the Pope in October 1187, must do penance for the sins which had provoked the catastrophe, at the same time preparing a new crusade to regain the Holy Places. Among the first to respond was Prince Richard, the famous 'Lionheart', while in January 1188 King Henry of England and King Philip of France swore to abandon their long feud and lead their united armies to Jerusalem. In token of their vow, they literally 'took the cross', accepting consecrated cloth crosses to be sewn upon the right shoulders of their cloaks. At that moment, reported chroniclers, the crusader symbol miraculously appeared in the sky above them, and all present ran forward to claim crosses of their own, of red cloth for the French but of shining white for the subjects of King Henry. Some, it was rumoured, even cut crosses in their flesh.

Amid further signs and portents, preparations for the expedition were at once put in hand. To finance it, Henry decreed the 'Saladin Tithe', the first ever income tax: excepting only those who personally took the cross, everyone must contribute a tenth of their

wealth. Lest sin mar the preparations, over-eating and luxurious clothes were forbidden by law, and no women were to follow the crusaders save 'washerwomen of unblemished reputation' — who must travel on foot, presumably to discourage less reputable ladies from infiltrating their ranks. Meanwhile, clergy all over Europe began raising the crusader army by 'preaching the cross', and Archbishop Baldwin of Canterbury decided on a recruiting tour of Wales, the home of the best archers and foot-soldiers in twelfth-century Britain. With him went his close friend Gerald, the court's leading expert on Welsh and Marcher affairs and no mean preacher himself.

In an age when few ordinary people travelled far from their homes and fewer still could read, preaching tours were much the best means of mass communication. Summoned by announcements in parish churches and market places, large crowds would gather at prearranged locations, waiting excitedly to see the famous visitors and hear their impassioned appeals for recruits, sometimes reinforced by lurid pictures of Saracens defiling Christ's tomb. Like the revival meetings of later centuries, therefore, crusading sermons could stir up collective emotions bordering on hysteria: miracles

Christ leading crusaders. From a thirteenth-century French manuscript Apocalypse (By permission of the British Library, Royal Ms. 19 B XV, f.37).

The crusader castle of Karak in Transjordan. One of the many new and powerful fortresses built during the Holy Wars, it was captured by Saladin's brother after an eight-month siege in 1188 (Photograph by R.D. Pringle).

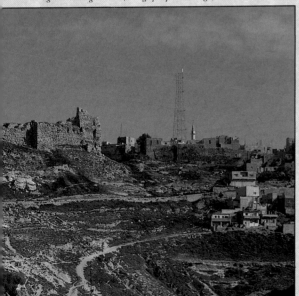

were even reported on several occasions when Baldwin preached, and at Haverfordwest he was almost trampled in the rush to secure cloth crosses.

Preaching the cross. A preacher hands a cloth cross to a king, while bishops and noblemen look on (By permission of the British Library, Royal Ms. 16 G VI, f.436v).

Elsewhere, however, men hesitated, or were forcibly restrained by their wives and friends. These knew well what taking the cross involved: a solemn vow to liberate the Holy Land, or die in the attempt; an expensive and hazardous journey, ending in fierce fighting. Nor could a promise made in the heat of the moment be easily set aside later. The names of cross-takers were carefully recorded, and stay-at-homes who failed to purchase a costly release from their vow risked excommunication, imprisonment or a ruinous fine. Long after 1188, indeed, fines were still being levied on those whose initial enthusiasm had been swamped by increasing age or growing families.

Others doubtless joined up after calculating the advantages, both present and future. On a practical level, this 'adventure for the sake of Christ crucified' offered crusaders the chance of plunder, immediate exemption from the onerous 'Saladin Tithe', and the suspension of all legal actions against them. A very much more powerful inducement, however, was the papal 'indulgence' absolving all those who took the cross from the every sin they had ever committed. Even the criminals who enlisted at Usk could thus make a completely fresh start, and if they died on crusade they were guaranteed a place in Heaven among the saints and martyrs. To many of those caught up in the crusading fervour of 1188, therefore, the cloth crosses distributed by Gerald and Baldwin represented the best bargain of their lives.

The Journey through Wales

The Travellers Set Out

Sunrise over Hereford, where Gerald's mission to Wales began and ended.

O ne morning during the first week of March 1188, a party of travellers rode westwards out of Hereford, bound for the Welsh border. No doubt they had prayed in the red sandstone Norman cathedral, for the solemn season of Lent — the forty days of fasting and penance preceding Easter — had just begun. But Lent is also a season of hope and endeavour, and thus a most appropriate time for their mission. During the next seven weeks they meant to ride round the four corners of Wales, recruiting for the great crusade which had fired all Europe with the hope of regaining the land of Christ's birth from the infidel.

In the cavalcade's place of honour rode a slight, swarthy figure with an honest, venerable face: Archbishop Baldwin of Canterbury, the mainspring of the mission. Born of humble Devon parents, this modest man of few and kindly words looked and acted like a learned Cistercian monk, which is what he had been until thrust unwillingly into the role of a busy church leader. According to Gerald, indeed, his gentleness and 'dovelike simplicity' made him a rather ineffectual archbishop, yet he was certainly no fool. During the coming journey through Wales, for example, he would go out of his way to celebrate Mass in every cathedral in the land, thus formally confirming his disputed authority over the Welsh clergy. He was also possessed of considerable fervour and courage. Deeply shocked by Saladin's capture of the Holy Cross (a relic to which he was personally devoted) he had been among the first to preach the Crusade in England, and he was destined for a hero's death before the walls of Moslem-held Acre.

Despite the glaring contrast between them, the archbishop was greatly attached to the forceful and flamboyant archdeacon of Brecon —

The Mission's Route through Wales

━━━━━ Route

- - - - Route conjectural

■ Overnight halts

□ Other places mentioned in text

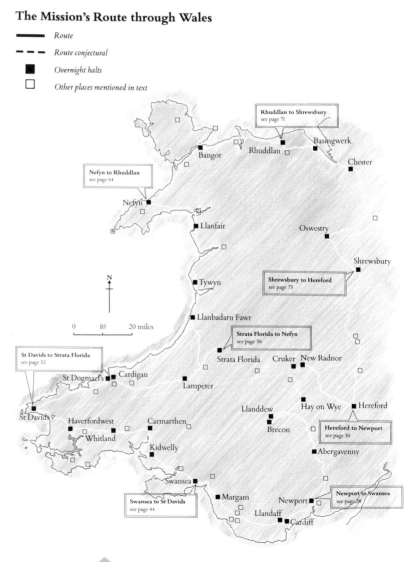

Rhuddlan to Shrewsbury see page 71

Nefyn to Rhuddlan see page 64

Shrewsbury to Hereford see page 75

Strata Florida to Nefyn see page 56

St Davids to Strata Florida see page 52

Hereford to Newport see page 30

Swansea to St Davids see page 44

Newport to Swansea see page 08

Basingwerk

Chester

Bangor

Rhuddlan

Oswestry

Shrewsbury

Nefyn

Llanfair

Tywyn

Llanbadarn Fawr

Strata Florida

Cruker

New Radnor

St Dogmael's

Cardigan

Lampeter

St Davids

Haverfordwest

Carmarthen

Llanddew

Hay on Wye

Hereford

Whitland

Kidwelly

Brecon

Abergavenny

Swansea

Margam

Newport

Llandaff

Cardiff

N

0   10   20 miles

'Of our travels via Hereford and Radnor'. The beginning of Gerald's Journey through Wales, *from an early fourteenth-century manuscript (By courtesy of the National Library of Wales, Ms. 3024C, f.4).*

his old friend Gerald de Barry, who now rode in his company, though not simply for companionship. As always, Gerald's principal asset was his extensive network of relationships with the rulers of Wales, and his most important duty would be to smooth over any diplomatic upsets the recruiting tour might provoke. He would also help with the preaching, and towards the end of the mission Baldwin suggested another task to him, that of chronicling the triumphant crusade which would surely follow. No doubt he knew that Gerald was already making rough notes for a description of their journey through Wales, and had probably been doing so ever since they left Hereford.

Gerald could likewise claim a professional acquaintance with the most distinguished of all the travellers, the great statesman Ranulf de Glanville, Chief Justiciar of England and so trusted a friend of Henry II that he was nicknamed 'the King's Eye'. De Glanville's time with the mission would be short, but Bishop Peter of St Davids would stay longer, and with him Gerald was on less happy terms. Peter had baulked him of St Davids in 1176, and since then they had quarrelled bitterly: yet under Baldwin's eye they kept the peace, and Gerald even wrote kindly of his former rival. Since neither Gerald nor Baldwin could speak fluent Welsh, an interpreter also accompanied the party — Alexander Cuhelyn, archdeacon of Bangor and a famous wit, who would translate the sermons they preached in Latin or Norman-French.

Though Gerald rarely mentions them, there must have been many more riders in the cavalcade. Doubtless there were armed guards, for prestige as well as protection, and there were certainly personal servants, including the monks who waited on the archbishop. Then there were mounted grooms, leading either spare riding horses (no-one could risk being immobilized by a sick or lame mount) or the still more essential pack ponies, laden with sturdy chests containing the mission's baggage. Gerald had only one extra horse to carry his vestments and precious books (later it almost drowned in the Neath quicksands) but Baldwin must have needed several, and there were probably at least as many packhorses as there were riders. Whether there were also baggage carts is much less certain. Since the travellers were generally to spend their nights in castles, towns, or monasteries, carts would not be needed to carry cumbersome beds and pavilions, and some of the mountain tracks and river crossings ahead would be quite impassable for wheeled vehicles. Even on the best medieval roads — hardly more than rough tracks by modern standards — carts could not keep up with ordinary riders, still less with riders travelling at the pace Gerald and Baldwin had to maintain.

The Journey through the Borderlands

New Radnor to Newport

At first the going was comparatively easy. By following a still serviceable Roman road (now the A438) across the Herefordshire plain, and then striking north-westwards through Kington, the travellers could have covered the thirty or so miles to their first objective in a single day. That

The border fortress of New Radnor survives as an impressive earthwork site.

objective was New Radnor — now no more than a quiet and attractive village, though still bounded by the ditch of its medieval defences and overshadowed by the great earthworks of its vanished castle. In 1188, however, Radnor was an important fortress on the boundary of Norman and Welsh-held territory, and here the mighty Prince Rhys ap Gruffudd, most influential of all the native rulers, had come to meet the archbishop. Though Rhys was currently Henry II's firm ally, there was at least a possibility that he might hinder Baldwin's progress, lest it strengthen the authority of the English over the Welsh church. Henry's right-hand man, de Glanville, had therefore come prepared to deal with this potentially delicate situation, while Gerald — Rhys's first cousin — was ready to add his persuasions. But in the event the prince gave the enterprise his

wholehearted support, and the archbishop preached his first crusading sermon in Wales.

Baldwin had scarcely finished speaking when Gerald threw himself down before him, seizing a cloth cross and vowing to join the crusade. He was thus the first man in Wales to do so, and his action was long premeditated: king, archbishop and de Glanville had all exhorted him to set this example, and (doubtless to his

The arms traditionally attributed to Ranulf de Glanville.

great satisfaction) he just managed to beat his rival Bishop Peter, who took the cross immediately afterwards. So, too, did Gerald's kinsman Einion o'r Porth — ruler of nearby Elfael and Rhys's son-in-law — and many other Welshmen likewise had the crusader symbol sewn to their cloaks, though Rhys himself was not among them. Apparently he had every intention of taking the vow in due course, but made the mistake of first returning home, where his wife 'turned aside his noble purpose by her womanly wiles'. All the same, at Radnor the mission had got off to a very promising start indeed.

Next morning de Glanville returned to England, his diplomatic work done, while the travellers moved on only a few miles to a place Gerald calls 'Cruker Castle'. This was all but certainly Castell Crug Eryr ('the eagle's crag'), whose spectacularly sited earthworks stand near the point where the A44 road plunges suddenly into the Edw valley, a mile north-west of the Fforest Inn at Llanfihangel Nant Melan. Here they stayed two nights, recruiting a brave but impoverished young man called Hector and (despite the tears and groans of his relations) Prince Maelgwyn ap Cadwallon of nearby Maelienydd — yet another of Gerald's cousins, who had witnessed his triumph at Llanbadarn church a dozen years earlier (p. 13).

Map: Hereford to Newport

Cruker · New Radnor · Glascwm · Hay on Wye · Glasbury · Hereford · Bronllys Castle · Llanddew · Brecon · Llanthony Priory · Llangorse Lake · River Usk · River Wye · Abergavenny · Usk Castle · Newport · Caerleon

0   10 miles

Legend:
— Route
- - - Route conjectural
† ▲ ▙ Overnight halts
□ Other places mentioned in text

The earthwork motte and bailey of Castell Crug Eryr ('the eagle's crag'), among the Radnorshire hills.

A handbell, presumably of the type once at Glascwm, from Llangwnadl, Gwynedd (By permission of the National Library of Wales).

Gerald, indeed, was now in country he knew very well, and his book changes its character. Instead of confining himself to describing the mission, henceforward he wanders off into long digressions about the 'noteworthy things' (usually meaning the natural or supernatural wonders) of the regions he passed through. Some of these stories he will have noted down at the time, having told or been told them as he rode along, or in the places where he lodged for the night; others he added much later (he was still revising his work twenty-five years afterwards) until they became so numerous that they often swamp the narrative of the mission altogether. Though they make the *Journey through Wales* exasperating as a pure travel guide, they also make it a much more readable book — which is just what Gerald would have wished.

The first set of stories probably sprang from a yarn-spinning session (perhaps at Cruker Castle) about the horrible calamities awaiting anyone who offended the local saints. The castellan of Radnor, for instance, had irreverently used the church of Llanafan Fawr (not far from Builth Wells) as a temporary kennel for his hounds — which promptly went mad, while he himself was struck blind. Those who denied their pennies to the miraculous boil-curing relic at St Harmons (near Rhayader) found

their boils breaking out again, while the huntsman who shot a freakish deer — a doe with stag's antlers — lost the sight of the eye he aimed with. Quite how he had offended Heaven is not clear, but the tale had the authority of the newly recruited crusader Einion o'r Porth, so it must have been true.

Engrossed in these wonders, Gerald fails to mention the travellers' route from Crug Eryr to their next destination, Hay-on-Wye. There is no obvious road through the intricate hills and valleys of southern Radnorshire, but they may well have journeyed via Glascwm, then the

St David's church, Glascwm, once the home of a miraculous handbell (By courtesy of the National Monuments Record, Wales).

most important church of the region and one said to have been founded by St David himself. Certainly Gerald tells a tale of the saint's magic 'bangu'

or handbell, taken from Glascwm and impiously seized by the garrison of Rhayader. Needless to say, Rhayader was forthwith burnt to the ground, saving only the wall where the 'bangu' hung. Today, curiously enough, Glascwm's fine late-medieval church displays another locally renowned bell, cracked from top to bottom after being hauled clean out of the belfry by over-enthusiastic wedding ringers.

Eventually they crossed the Wye and entered Hay, where the crusading sermon provoked an extraordinary scene. Many of the townsmen were intent on taking the cross, but their equally obdurate wives and friends held them back by their clothes: not to be deterred, the recruits simply slipped off the hindering garments, running in what was left to seek refuge with Baldwin in the castle. Whichever of Hay's two Norman fortresses this was — the mound by the church or the stronger and later stone castle above the market place — the party stayed there overnight, before travelling south-westwards up the Wye valley towards Brecon.

The Norman 'keep' of Hay Castle, built by Matilda de Braose, stands above the market place.

Passing the River Llynfi (which warned of invasions by turning bright green) at Glasbury, towards evening they rode into Llanddew for another night's rest.

Now Gerald was really at home. For Llanddew, a mile or so north-east of Brecon, was his official residence as archdeacon, and there he had:

'. . . a little house and dwelling . . . well fitted for my studies and labours. It always gives me great pleasure, and brings thoughts of Paradise. I much prefer it to all the riches of Croesus, and value it above all the transitory things of this world'.

As we know from his letters, it was not as modest as all that (it had a courtyard garden, a good set of stables, and a productive home farm) but by Tudor times it had already 'fallen doune for the more part', and now it has vanished completely. Still to be seen, however, are the remains of the neighbouring bishop's palace — a pretty arched gateway, a well and the shattered shell of a hall — where the travellers probably stayed in 1188, and the high-gabled, severely attractive church (much altered since

The arms of William de Braose.

The east end of the priory church at Brecon (now Brecon Cathedral), begun by William de Braose in 1201.

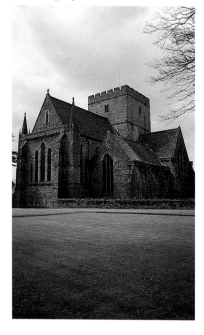

Llanddew church at Gerald's official residence as archdeacon of Brecon.

Gerald's time) outside which Baldwin doubtless preached his sermon. This done, Gerald took the opportunity to present the archbishop with some light reading, his own 'not undistinguished' Topography of Ireland. So delighted was Baldwin, reported

The Ely Tower at Brecon, de Braose's castle keep above the Honddu.

the proud author, that he read or heard a passage from it on every succeeding day of their journey.

That journey next took them to populous Brecon, where they presumably recruited more men. Gerald, however, was more interested in writing about William de Braose, the lord not only of Brecon but also of Radnor, Hay and Abergavenny, and indeed the most powerful, ruthless and hated of all the Marcher barons. Either because he feared or genuinely liked his mighty neighbour, Gerald very quickly skated over de Braose's notorious misdeeds, concentrating instead on his piety. Whenever he spoke, he always mentioned God first, ('Please God', 'If God Wills it', 'In God's name let it be done') he never so much as glimpsed a church without saying a prayer, and he deliberately sought blessings from passing children. His wife Matilda, Gerald added, was an excellent woman, prudent, chaste, and a marvellous housekeeper — an astoundingly flattering estimate of that formidable lady, whose fearsome reputation as a baby-eating, demon-conjuring witch persisted in Breconshire seven centuries after she starved to death in King John's dungeons.

Evidence of de Braose's piety and military power can still be seen in Brecon, for it was he who began the beautiful east end of the cathedral, with its slender early Gothic lancet windows, and who built the 'Ely Tower' — a fragmentary shell keep — on the steep castle mound guarding the Honddu bridge. Possibly the travellers stayed hereabouts, but at this point Gerald became so immersed in the manifold wonders of the region that he lost the thread of his narrative altogether. Instead, he poured out a torrent of tales of vengeful saints and of mysterious Llangorse Lake (p. 81), of the frenzied dancing in St Eluned's churchyard, and of King Arthur's throne between the twin peaks of the Brecon Beacons. Still more remarkably, he assures us, a crowd of onlookers had witnessed a local knight giving birth to a calf, after three years of painful labour.

There seems little doubt, however, that the mission's route from Brecon passed close to Bronllys Castle. Its tall cylindrical keep belongs to a slightly later date, but the enormous mound on which it stands existed in 1188, when the castle belonged to Walter de Clifford — incidentally the father of Henry II's mistress 'the Fair Rosamund', whom Gerald disapprovingly called 'shameless Rosie' (p. 18). With great relish, Gerald relates how a wicked knight named Mahel met his end there. As a divine punishment for persecuting the bishop of St Davids (who happened to be Gerald's uncle) he was struck down by a stone which fell from a tower during a fire: believing it to have been hurled by St David in person, he died begging the bishop's forgiveness.

The early thirteenth-century round keep at Bronllys Castle stands on an earlier earthen mound.

The travellers were now bound for Abergavenny, and much the easiest road ran to the east of the Black Mountains, down the Rhiangoll and Usk valleys and past Tretower (with its unique grouping of castle and later manor house, the best surviving medieval monument of the region). Why Baldwin's party did not follow this route (and likewise ignored the track down the Vale of Ewyas, via Llanthony Priory) is by no means obvious. Instead, they chose 'the narrow overgrown path called the evil pass of Coit Wroneu, or Wroneu Wood' — a track which climbs to over two thousand feet above Talgarth, and then drops down into the heavily wooded ravine of the Grwyne Fawr stream. This most difficult of the Black Mountain passes was apparently an established twelfth-century routeway, though its dangers were not all natural ones. Fifty or so years earlier, Gerald relates, Lord Richard de Clare of Cardigan had light-heartedly dismissed his escort and ridden along it unarmed, accompanied only by the merry tunes of his minstrel and fiddler. His Welsh enemies, waiting concealed in the undergrowth, leapt out and cut him to pieces. According to tradition, he was murdered at the place still called

Llanthony Priory, in its steep-sided valley, amid the wild country of the Black Mountains.

Coed-Dias ('the wood of revenge'): nearby is the remote and atmospheric little church of Partrishow, where (again according to local tradition) Gerald and Baldwin stopped to preach in 1188.

By following the Coed Grwyne track, they had passed two miles west of 'the noble monastery of Llanthony, environed by its hills' and concealed from their view by a high ridge. Yet Gerald devotes a whole chapter to it, one of the most lyrical in his book, and he clearly knew and loved Llanthony. What impressed him most was its healthy climate and beautiful natural setting ('The entire treasury of the realm', an earlier traveller had remarked, 'is not sufficient to build such a cloister') but he also admired its fine church, just then in the course of reconstruction. Combining traditionally Norman round arches with the pointed arches of the newly-fashionable Gothic style, the eastern and central portions of this church still remain much as he knew them, while its setting is no less magnificent eight centuries later.

As Gerald reported at length, however, even paradisal Llanthony had its troubles. Founded by two isolation-seeking hermits early in the twelfth century, it had originally been a shining example of holy poverty and simplicity. Then an outbreak of border warfare forced its Augustinian 'black canons' to flee to Gloucester, and things began to go wrong: safe in their new Gloucester house ('Llanthony the second') the increasingly corrupt and Anglicized canons had stripped their Welsh mother church of its books and ornaments, and only now was it regaining its former glory. Gerald's grudge against the emigrant Gloucester canons, possibly dating from his early days at the rival Gloucester monastery of St Peter's, launched him on a wholesale criticism of monks in general. The Cistercians, though hard-working and abstemious, were over-greedy for land; the proud Benedictines were far too rich; while the Cluniacs were

'The entire treasury of the realm is not sufficient to build such a cloister'. The hills around Llanthony Priory, seen through its nave arches.

Gerald thought the Cistercians hard working but greedy. A Cistercian lay brother reaping corn from an early twelfth-century manuscript (By courtesy of Bibliothèque Municipale, Dijon, Ms. 170, f.59).

Fourteenth-century fortifications at Abergavenny Castle, scene of twelfth-century Norman treachery and Welsh revenge.

nothing but feckless, spendthrift gluttons. If only they would imitate the humble, pious, unambitious Augustinians of Llanthony, how much better they would be. 'But we must return to our business', as Gerald rather guiltily remarked at this point.

Having arrived in Abergavenny, the mission recruited many crusaders, including a hesitant local nobleman who wanted to consult his friends first: when Baldwin advised him to ask his wife's permission as well, he was shamed into an immediate vow. It is perhaps surprising that they did not encounter more distrust, for during recent years Abergavenny had seen much bloody treachery. In 1175, William de Braose had invited the seven leading Welsh landowners of Gwent to its castle, under sworn oath of safe-conduct. Once inside and disarmed, they were all murdered out of hand, and their killers rampaged plundering and slaying through their lands, slaughtering even the infant son of Seisyll ap Dyfnwal in his mother's arms. Seven years later, however, the surviving sons and grandsons of the dead men took their revenge. Concealing themselves and their ladders in an overgrown castle ditch, they waited until the garrison's vigilance faltered and then scaled the palisades, killing or capturing all within and burning the wooden fortress to the ground: only the keep held out, though Welsh arrowheads penetrated its four-finger thick oaken door.

Whitewashing de Braose once again, Gerald rather unconvincingly denies that he was actually responsible for the massacre — though he admittedly might have prevented it, had not the murdered men themselves recently slain his uncle Henry. The scene of the crime, Abergavenny Castle, still occupies its strong site above the Usk water-meadows: its sadly ruined walls and towers date from long after de Braose's time, but the ditch which concealed the Welsh avengers can still be seen.

Rather more remains of Usk Castle, ten easy miles south-east of Abergavenny and the travellers' next goal. Its little rectangular Norman keep, set in a circuit of later walls within tremendous tree-grown

The much-altered Norman keep of Usk Castle, where criminals and murderers took the cross in 1188 (Photograph by Peter Humphries).

earthworks, stands in a delightful private garden high above Usk town, and its courtyard witnessed an amazing event in 1188. For among the many recruits who took the cross were some of the most notorious bandits and murderers of the region, persuaded to wipe away their sins by the sermons of Baldwin and their local bishop, William Saltmarsh of Llandaff. 'That good and honest man' — high praise from Gerald — thereafter joined the mission as it continued southward, crossing the Usk river near the ancient Roman ruins of Caerleon.

Caerleon, 'the city of the Legion' and once the principal Roman fortress of south Wales, filled Gerald with wonder. Still remarkably impressive today, its ruins were far more extensive in the twelfth century, and though part of his description of its former golden-roofed magnificence was lifted straight from Geoffrey of Monmouth's

contemporary 'historical' romance, Gerald saw for himself,

'. . . its extraordinary hot baths and remnants of temples and theatres, all enclosed by splendid walls, parts of which yet remain standing. Everywhere you look, both within and without this circuit of defences, are subterranean constructions, water conduits and underground passages: but what I consider most notable of all are the stoves built with amazing skill, which once transmitted heat through narrow pipes hidden in the walls'.

Caerleon's fascinating Roman baths, amphitheatre and modern museum still testify to the accuracy of Gerald's pioneering archaeological observations, but his version of its post-Roman history is considerably less reliable. Saints Aaron and Julius, he truthfully tells us, were martyred there, but that 'Saint' Amphibalus was born there is doubtful, since that

'Extraordinary hot baths'. The Roman Natatio, or bathing pool at the Caerleon Fortress Baths.

Torturers martyr the mythical St Amphibalus of Caerleon, by winding his intestines around a tree. From a thirteenth-century manuscript (By courtesy of the British Library, Royal Ms. 2 B VI, f.10v).

entirely mythical figure owed his origin to a misreading of the Latin word for 'cloak'. Gerald also believed that King Arthur had held court at Caerleon, and indeed he was keen to reinforce the very dubious notion that it had once been the capital of Christian Wales, with an independent archbishop of its own. From here it was but a short step to the really important point about Caerleon. In accordance with Merlin's prophecy, its archbishop's authority had allegedly been handed over to St David, and thus the bishops of St Davids were now the rightful leaders of an independent Welsh Church. As he rode on to Newport, Gerald may well have dreamt of becoming such a leader himself.

The Roman amphitheatre at Caerleon, traditionally but misleadingly known as King Arthur's Round Table.

Gerald, King Arthur, and the Legendary History of Britain

by Huw Pryce

As Gerald contemplated the Roman ruins at Caerleon in 1188, Geoffrey of Monmouth's *History of the Kings of Britain* cannot have been far from his mind. Completed some fifty years earlier, Geoffrey's book had been an instant success. It provided the first coherent narrative of the early history of the Britons and introduced Arthur to an international audience. According to Geoffrey, it was at Caerleon that Arthur had held court, exhibiting the highest virtues of chivalry. Gerald alluded to this in the *Journey*, but how much of Geoffrey's work he believed is unclear. A little later in the same chapter he recounts how the seer Meilyr was relieved from the torments of demons by having St John's Gospel placed on his chest, only to be afflicted again more grievously when Geoffrey's *History* was put there in its place!

Gerald accepted that Arthur had been a great king of the Britons, whose renown was reflected in the name *Caer Arthur*, 'the fortress of Arthur', the highest peak of the Brecon Beacons (Pen-y-Fan today). Yet he also realized that virtually nothing was reliably known about what Arthur had done, citing the explanation given by the Welsh that Gildas, the sixth-century British churchman, had thrown all his writings on the king into the sea. Most of what was said about Arthur was therefore legend rather than history.

Caer Arthur — 'the fortress of Arthur', in the Brecon Beacons.

A page from a late twelfth-century manuscript of Geoffrey of Monmouth's History of the Kings of Britain. *The book was well-known to Gerald. It was a great success, and introduced King Arthur to an international audience (By courtesy of Burgerbibliothek, Bern, Ms. 568, f.18).*

A leaden mortuary cross, alleged to be from the tomb of King Arthur at Glastonbury, but now lost. From William Camden's Britannia *(1610). In two of his works, Gerald tells us he saw the cross himself and traced the lettering which was cut into it.*

One such legend was that Arthur would return and lead the Welsh in recovering their rightful sovereignty over the whole island of Britain. For Gerald, this belief was foolish, and he had the evidence to disprove it. Not long after his journey round Wales a dramatic discovery was made at Glastonbury Abbey: the monks had excavated between two pyramids in

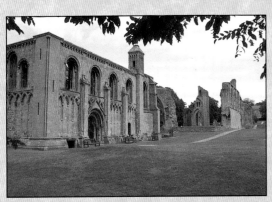

The Benedictine abbey at Glastonbury, Somerset, where about 1190 the monks 'excavated' what were thought to be the bodies of Arthur and Queen Guinevere. Gerald appears to have visited Glastonbury and inspected the remains himself (Photograph by David Robinson).

Arthur's Stone, Cefn Bryn, Gower — a prehistoric chambered tomb. One of the many sites associated in legend with King Arthur.

their cemetery and, sixteen feet down, found an oak containing what were thought to be the bodies of Arthur and Queen Guinevere. Gerald subsequently saw these and wrote two accounts of the exhumation, noting the huge size of Arthur's bones and describing how a lock of Guinevere's fair hair had crumbled into dust when grabbed by an over-eager monk. The discovery thus gave substance to the legends about Arthur while depriving them of any dangerous political implications: the much vaunted deliverer of the Welsh was well and truly dead.

The conviction that Arthur would return was grounded, however, in a powerful tradition of political prophecy associated with another figure of the legendary past — Merlin (Myrddin). According to Gerald, there had been two Merlins — one, Merlin Ambrosius, found as a child at Carmarthen which

was named after him (Caerfyrddin — Caer + Myrddin) and who later prophesied to Vortigern at Dinas Emrys (see p. 68), and another, Merlin Silvester, struck mad in a Scottish forest in the time of Arthur. Both Merlins had foretold the future fate of the Britons, and Gerald quoted some of their prophecies, regarding them as valid historical evidence which subsequent events had vindicated. He also boasted that he had had Merlin Silvester's prophecies translated into Latin from an old Welsh book which he had found at Nefyn during his journey in 1188. Nevertheless, Gerald could be critical as well as credulous in his attitude to such prophecies. He firmly rejected the view held by many Welsh people in his day that Merlin's predictions were about to be fulfilled, that foreign occupation of Britain would cease and the Britons would exult once more in their ancient name and power in the island: that moment had not yet come. What Gerald could not deny, however, was the popular appeal and power of such beliefs, fuelled by a historical tradition that combined a vision of a splendid if ultimately tragic past with the hope of an even more glorious future.

The medieval view of Arthur. A scene from an Arthurian romance — the king leaves Camelot (By permission of the British Library, Additional Ms. 10293, f.35).

The Journey through South Wales
Newport to St Davids

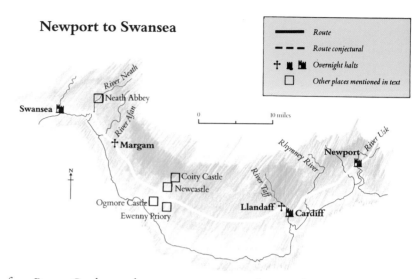

Route

Route conjectural

Overnight halts

Other places mentioned in text

Swansea

River Neath

Neath Abbey

River Afan

Margam

River Usk

Rhymney River

Newport

River Taff

Coity Castle
Newcastle

Ogmore Castle
Ewenny Priory

Llandaff

Cardiff

0   10 miles

At Newport, Baldwin and Gerald changed direction, entering a new kind of country. Previously they had journeyed south through the border hills, but now they would ride westward along the coastal plain, often following the Roman road called the Portway, 'the way between towns' which led from Caerleon via Cardiff to Carmarthen. Yet the going would not always be easy, for instead of mountain passes they now had to negotiate a whole succession of streams, rivers and estuaries, with their shifting fords and hazardous quicksands. Most of these river crossings were guarded by Norman castles, and the Norman grip was more firmly established on the south Wales lowlands than on the border uplands they had just traversed. Today, too, the heavily populated coastal strip between Newport and Swansea presents a marked contrast to the rural borderlands, for here the Industrial Revolution has set its mark more indelibly than on any other part of Wales. Sometimes, therefore, it seems hard to envisage the region as Gerald saw it eight hundred years ago: but a surprising number of the buildings he knew still remain, and they are well worth seeking out.

At first sight, for example, modern Newport preserves little of Gerald's time, and even the imposing castle ruins by the Usk bridge date from the later Middle Ages. On the hill above the castle, however, stands the partly Norman church of St Woolos (now the cathedral) where Baldwin may have preached his successful crusading sermon. Within, opening into the fine Norman nave, is a splendidly carved Norman archway supported on free-standing Classical columns, said to have been brought

from Roman Caerleon and recut to suit Norman taste.

The splendid Norman nave arch at St Woolos Cathedral, Newport, with its Classical columns (By courtesy of the National Monuments Record, Wales).

'Woolos' is an Anglicization of 'Gwynllyw', patron saint of the region of Gwynllŵg or Wentloog: bound for Cardiff, the travellers crossed its marshes next day, fording with some difficulty the winding Nant Pencarn stream. Twenty-five years earlier, Gerald recalled, Henry II had passed the same way on campaign against Rhys ap Gruffudd, closely observed by the local population. Merlin, they knew, had prophesied that if a strong man with freckles (a good description of Henry) crossed the stream by the ancient ford of Rhyd Pencarn, the Welsh would be beaten. That ford was long disused, but when the king

came to the normal crossing place, his horse shied at a fanfare of welcoming trumpets from the opposite bank, and he angrily turned aside to splash across omen-haunted Rhyd Pencarn instead. At this the watchers despaired, and sure enough Rhys surrendered soon afterwards.

Nine years later, according to Gerald, Henry himself received a fateful warning hereabouts. Just as he was leaving a chapel, he suddenly encountered what appeared to be a gaunt, white-robed English priest, who solemnly commanded him to forbid all Sunday trading throughout his realms. Since the king's English was not very good, he needed an interpreter to ask 'this yokel' whether he had been dreaming. The apparition testily replied that unless he heeded the warning, and generally mended his ways, he would soon hear bad news that would haunt him all his life. It then immediately disappeared, and within the year Henry heard that his sons had revolted against him.

This incident happened at St Piran's chapel (itself long vanished) in Cardiff, whose 'noble castle on the river Taff' was the mission's next stopping place. Though now almost overshadowed by the fantastic clustering towers of Lord Bute's adjacent Victorian-Gothic palace, the core of Cardiff Castle remains much as Gerald knew it — a polygonal

Cardiff Castle's powerful Norman keep, on its moated mound.

shell-keep on a forty-foot-high moated mound, within the reused outer defences of a large Roman fort. William the Conqueror had probably raised the mound during his visit to Wales in 1081, and during the second quarter of the following century Earl Robert of Gloucester added the stone keep, the headquarters and chief strongpoint of Norman power in Glamorgan. Yet all its strength and importance, Gerald noted, did not prevent Robert's son, Earl William, from suffering a most humiliating experience there. By confiscating some of his lands, William had offended Ifor Bach of Senghennydd, 'a man of small stature but immense boldness'. Despite the fact that the castle was guarded by over a hundred men-at-arms and a still larger number of archers, Ifor managed to scale the walls by night and snatch the earl and his family from their beds. Spiriting them away to his native woodlands he refused to release them until they restored the stolen estates, with a few more for good measure.

After a rather less disturbed night's sleep in the castle, the travellers moved on across the river to preach in Llandaff, traditionally at the cross which still stands on the cathedral green. Their hearers were carefully segregated, the English standing on one side and the Welsh on the other, and presumably sermons were preached in both languages, for 'many from both nations' made the crusading vow. Next morning, following what was clearly an agreeable stay with Bishop William Saltmarsh, Baldwin ceremonially said Mass at the high altar of Llandaff Cathedral, part of his plan to confirm his authority over every Welsh diocese. The fine Norman arch behind the altar where he stood (together with two Norman doorways into Llandaff's nave) has survived all the cathedral's later troubles, including the landmine which gutted it so disastrously in 1941.

As they rode westwards out of Llandaff along the Portway (hereabouts still in use as the A48)

The Norman south nave doorway of Llandaff Cathedral.

Gerald de Barry remembered Barry Island, the ancestral home of his family a few miles to the south. There, as he no doubt informed his companions, stood the ivy-covered chapel of St Baroc, its patron saint, and if you put your ear to a certain rock, you could hear a noise like the hammering of blacksmiths below.

Further west, they passed or perhaps halted briefly at 'the little cell of Ewenny' — a cell being an outpost of a larger monastery, in this case Gerald's old school, St Peter's Abbey at Gloucester. Modern travellers should certainly not pass Ewenny Priory too quickly, for it preserves one of the most remarkable complexes of medieval buildings in south Wales.

The tomb-slab of Maurice de Londres, founder of Ewenny Priory and defender of Kidwelly Castle.

The south transept of Ewenny Priory church, displaying zigzag decoration.

The cavernous eastern sections of its fortress-like church display Norman architecture at its most sternly powerful, relieved only by bands of zigzag decoration: there, too, is the original stone altar table and the unusual founder's monument, inscribed 'Here lies Maurice de Londres, the founder. God reward him for his labour'. More surprising, however, are the towers and gatehouses of the priory's fortified perimeter wall, making it appear more like a stronghold than a house of religion. Why these defences were built is not clear. Perhaps they were merely for show, but Ewenny may also have formed a makeshift link in the chain of stronger castles — Ogmore to the west, Newcastle Bridgend and Coity to the north — which guarded the Glamorgan lowlands.

Probably the mission crossed the Ewenny river near the priory, though they may have done so a mile further west, where Ogmore Castle's early Norman keep and 'ringwork' still watch over a line of stepping stones. At any rate, their destination was the great Cistercian abbey of Margam, renowned for its limitless charity to pilgrims and the local poor. Even Gerald (not normally over-fond of monks) was tremendously impressed, and he relates several wonders which plainly demonstrated God's favour towards the abbey.

A young man who fired one of its barns died raving mad, crying that 'his insides were all burnt up'; another who struck a blow within its precinct was slain on the very same spot; and, most miraculous of all, a monastic cornfield suddenly ripened a month before harvest-time, enabling the monks to feed the famine-stricken crowd at their gates. Though picturesquely sited against a backdrop of wooded crags, Margam's remains

Ogmore Castle, guarding the crossing of the Ewenny river, has one of the earliest Norman keeps in south Wales.

are now comparatively scanty: part of the church, encased in a Georgian successor; a twelve-sided Gothic chapter house; and a fine collection of early Christian monuments in the adjacent Stones Museum.

God's favour towards Margam Abbey was displayed by a miraculous harvest in time of famine. A fourteenth-century scene from the Luttrell Psalter (By permission of the British Library, Additional Ms. 42130, f.172v).

Although much altered, the west front of Margam Abbey church still retains its Norman character.

The notable collection of early Christian monuments in Margam Stones Museum.

Next day the travellers had an extremely alarming experience. Bound for Swansea and guided by Prince Morgan ap Caradog, they set out along the shoreline to cross the tidal rivers Afan and Neath. They had chosen a particularly bad time to do so, for according to the Margam chronicle, 'the, sea rose up much higher than usual' in [the] March [of] 1188, 'so that innumerable beasts of all kinds were drowned in many places, and quite a few people were also swept away'. Fording the Afan was bad enough, but the Neath had an even worse reputation for inaccessibility,

'because of its dangerous quicksands, which suddenly suck down everything placed upon them. One of our packhorses [the only one possessed by the writer of these lines] was trotting along the lower road near the sea, and although it was in the middle of a group of others, it alone was nearly plunged into the abyss. Eventually it was pulled out, with great difficulty and after much hard and dangerous work by the horse-boys, though not without damage to my books and belongings. Although we had Morgan, the leading man of those parts, as our guide, we only reached the river after suffering many perils, and even more falls. Of course, fear of the unknown made us hurry through these quicksands, despite the warnings of our guide, for "Terror gave us wings": but in this kind of dangerous situation, as we found out at the time, it is far better to go carefully and quite slowly'.

After their scare, they had no intention of wading the river itself, whose fords shifted with the tides and could not be found at all following heavy rain. So they crossed by boat instead, (probably at Briton Ferry), thus passing well south of the Cistercian abbey of Neath, and at last reached Swansea. Clearly their adventure provided them with conversation for days to come. Many years later, indeed, Gerald remembered an exchange between two of Baldwin's attendant monks, discussing the perils of the journey. 'It's a hard country this', remarked one. 'Not at all', quipped the other, thinking of the quicksands, 'yesterday we found it much too soft'.

continued on page 44

The Hazards of Travel

A section of the Sarn Helen between Llanddewi Brefi and Llanbadarn Fawr (see p. 57). During the Middle Ages, such older Roman roads provided ready routeways (Photograph by Terry James, by permission of the Dyfed Archaeological Trust).

Quicksands were only one of the many hazards that faced the twelfth-century traveller: hazards which must have been only too familiar to Gerald, who spent a great deal of time on the road. Quite apart from his journey through Wales with Baldwin, his official travels as archdeacon, and his diplomatic missions as a courtier, he is known to have visited Paris at least three times and Ireland on four occassions, as well as making four journeys to distant Rome — during his struggle for St Davids, indeed, he was more or less continuously in transit for over three years. Travel, then, was very much a part of everyday life for him, as it was for many men of his class — King John shifted his residence an average of twelve times a month throughout his reign, dragging his entourage with him, and few aristocrats or senior churchmen stayed still for long. Yet all this journeying had some purpose — war, diplomacy, business or pilgrimage — and travel was far too risky and uncomfortable to undertake merely for pleasure.

To the medieval mind, indeed, travel was virtually synonymous with hardship, and a handbook of useful Latin phrases compiled for tenth century Welsh pilgrims conveys a vivid picture of the wayfarer's day:

> 'Get up, friend, wake from your accustomed sleep. Fasten your belt, so that we can get on the road early, for the day is short and the way is long'.

> 'Give me my cloak, give me my shoes, hand me my staff to support me'.

> 'O brother, show us the right road, if you can'.

> 'Have you heard whether there are any footpads or robbers on this road?'

> 'Boy, light us a fire, and do it quickly, for I am worn out by the labour of the journey, and by the very long, very muddy road, full of swamps and foulness'.

> 'Give us warm water, we must wash our feet before sleeping'.

Fortunately, there were some consolations.

> 'Innkeeper, bring us a pot of ale, or wine, or cider, or mead'.

> 'O best of girls, give me a kiss'.

Unlike such pedestrian wayfarers, of course, Gerald invariably travelled on horseback, taking care to obtain the best mounts he could afford and to look after them well: the ill-treatment of horses infuriated him. Yet he still had to contend with the weather, and it is hard to believe that Baldwin's mission did not suffer at least one really foul day while riding through Wales in the early spring of 1188. The March of that year, indeed, saw exceptionally severe flooding in the Margam area. Admittedly, Gerald never mentions the weather in his account, and elsewhere he declares that it is unmanly to take any notice of it at all. This was mere Geraldian bravado. For as every medieval traveller knew, heavy rain would make fords (like that of the Neath) impassable, and transform unmetalled roads into muddy swamps, while snow could block mountain passes for months on end.

Even in fine weather, the roads of twelfth-century Wales were execrable by modern standards. The best (assuming they were still kept in some kind of repair) were probably old Roman roads like the Portway in the south or Sarn Helen in the west, or the routes maintained as an act of charity by roadside monasteries like Margam and Strata Florida. Among the worst must have been the upland tracks the mission sometimes traversed, like the 'evil pass' of Coit Wroneu in the Black Mountains, or 'Evil Street' in the Shropshire hills. In an age when maps were virtually non-existent, moreover, deciding on the right road to follow could be a serious problem: Baldwin's eminence ensured that guides were always on hand for the mission, but later in his career Gerald was unable to find anyone to direct him through the wilderness of the Cambrian Mountains. Local advice was absolutely essential when it came to locating river-fords or negotiating quicksands, though there seems to have been an established ferry service across some of the wider Welsh estuaries, and the ferry boats must have been big enough to accommodate the mission's mounts and packhorses.

Seagoing boats, indeed, were much the easiest means of travel between the coastal settlements of Wales, as well as probably the safest. For the hazards which beset Welsh roads were not all meteorological or geographical — as was starkly demonstrated by the freshly-murdered corpse the mission found near St Clears. A decade later, Gerald's horses and money-chests were seized by Welsh bandits near Builth, while his writings abound in tales of ambushes, assassinations and highway robbery. All prudent travellers therefore went armed — Richard de Clare, who preferred minstrels to bodyguards, paid the price of his folly in Coit Wroneu — and though church law theoretically prohibited priests from carrying weapons, Gerald himself possessed a sword of the finest Lombardy steel.

The most feared roads, then, were those which passed through woods or scrubland, all too convenient a lurking place for footpads or assassins. When Edward I invaded Wales in the thirteenth century, he employed gangs of woodcutters to clear a safe path for his armies, and he later ordered that main roads should be stripped of undergrowth for two hundred feet on either side, to foil the 'sackpurses and roberdesmen' who 'are accustomed to crouch by the highway, lying in wait to beat, maim, rob and slay the people'. Thick forest, very much more extensive in medieval than in modern Wales, might also harbour wolves, particularly dangerous

during hard winters. Gerald mentions them several times, and his friend Walter Map tells of a Welsh traveller who was slain by them, after being driven out into a snowstorm by his host's scolding wife.

Such a breach of hospitality, however, was exceptional, for the hazards and inconveniences of travel through twelfth-century Wales were counterbalanced by the universal kindness of its people. 'Everyone's home is open to all', declared Gerald in his *Description of Wales*.

> '. . . and there is no need for travellers even to ask for accommodation. You just walk straight into the house and hand over your weapons for safekeeping: then someone immediately offers you water, and if you wash your feet, that means you intend to stay the night'.

So polite were Welsh hosts, added Map, that for the three days they never presumed to ask a visitor who he was, or where he had come from: in a land where blood-feuds were common, it was perhaps better not to know. Visitors, moreover, thought nothing of eating (and drinking) their hosts out of house and home, and there was no limit to the appetite of a hungry Welsh traveller with his feet under someone else's table.

Leaving south Wales and the territories of the Lord Rhys, the mission of 1188 crossed the Dovey estuary into the mountainous north (see pp. 57, 62). This artist's impression of the episode serves as a reminder of the many such rivers and estuaries travellers in medieval Wales would frequently encounter (Illustration by Ivan Lapper).

None the worse for their fright amid the Neath quicksands, on the morning following their arrival in Swansea the travellers gathered many more recruits, all anxious to wipe away their sins by taking the cross. An old man named Cador, however, sought to win the same benefit by another means. He was too weak and infirm, he said, to travel to Jerusalem, but if he contributed a tenth of his

Swansea's late medieval castle lies just to the south of its Norman predecessor.

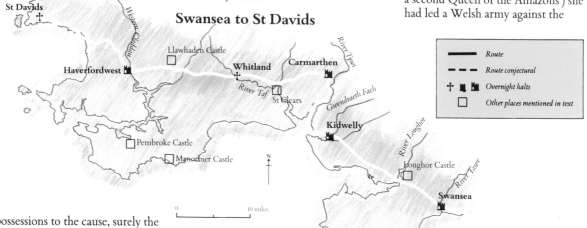

Swansea to St Davids

——	Route
– – –	Route conjectural
✝ 🏰	Overnight halts
☐	Other places mentioned in text

possessions to the cause, surely the archbishop would forgive him at least half his sins? Such bargains were an established method of raising funds for the crusade, and Baldwin agreed. Then, after a little thought, Cador put forward another proposition. If one-tenth of his goods would nullify half his transgressions, then logically a second tenth would nullify the other half, leaving him as free from sin as if he had actually joined the crusade. Smiling at his 'devout cunning', Baldwin could not help embracing the old man, though Gerald does not tell us whether he agreed to his request.

During their second evening in Swansea, Gerald had time to remember the tale of Elidyr and the fairies (p. 85). Where they stayed is unknown, and the castle in the city centre belongs to a later date, its distinctive multi-arched parapet being the hallmark of the fourteenth-century builder — Bishop Henry de Gower of St Davids. Next day, the mission rode on through the open

country at the neck of the Gower peninsula before fording the Loughor estuary — probably at Loughor town, where a single ruined medieval tower stands on a roadside mound, raised on

The scanty remains of Loughor Castle.

one corner of the old Roman fort of *Leucarum*. Then, entering the Carmarthenshire district of modern Dyfed, they pushed on across the Gwendraeth Fawr and Gwendraeth Fach rivers and into Kidwelly.

Though the magnificent and well-preserved castle which still dominates Kidwelly is the work of the thirteenth to fifteenth centuries, its outer walls stand on the massive D-shaped rampart of the earlier fortress where the travellers stayed in 1188. Doubtless they also preached a sermon here, but Gerald was keen to tell the story of the redoubtable Gwenllian, mother of Rhys ap Gruffudd and a distant relation of his own. Some half-century before ('like a second Queen of the Amazons') she had led a Welsh army against the Kidwelly Normans, so certain of victory that she brought her two young sons to share in it. Instead, the Welsh were routed by Maurice de Londres near the farm later called Maes Gwenllian ('Gwenllian's field') and in the battle she herself was stabbed and beheaded.

This same Maurice de Londres was also the founder of Ewenny Priory, but according to Gerald he was both credulous and grasping in his private life. 'As always' (declared the misogynistic Gerald) 'the wife was well aware of the husband's failings', and with the help of her servants she decided to play a trick on him. Sick of hearing about his precious stags, she persuaded him that they were eating his equally precious sheep — proving her point by displaying two dissected deer carcasses, their stomachs carefully lined with wool.

Kidwelly — one of the finest castles in Wales. The crescent-shaped rampart of an earlier fortress, where Gerald stayed in 1188, can clearly be seen beneath its outer defences.

At Kidwelly the travellers temporarily changed their mode of transport, sailing northwards up the broad Tywi estuary in a ship and 'leaving on our left hand side the castles of Llanstephan and Laugharne, set on rocky crags above the sea'. By the time Gerald wrote up his notes a year or so later, both these castles had been stormed and taken by Rhys ap Gruffudd. Both still survive (though the earth and timber fortresses of Gerald's day were subsequently rebuilt in stone) and both are outstandingly picturesque. Then they

'Set on a rocky crag above the sea'. The much-disputed and much-rebuilt Llanstephan Castle.

hurried on to Carmarthen, perhaps taking the road from the usual landing place at 'Green Castle' near Llangain. Gerald believed that Carmarthen was Caer Myrddin,

An aerial view of Carmarthen, where the fossilized outline of Roman Moridunum *has left its mark on the planning of the later town (Photograph by Terry James, by courtesy of the Dyfed Archaeological Trust).*

'Merlin's Town', and that the prophet had been found there as a child, the offspring of a demon and a mortal woman. In fact, its name ('Caer Moridun') derives from its origin as the Roman town of *Moridunum*, whose walls were still partly visible when Gerald passed. He tells us, however, nothing about what the mission did there, for his attention was fixed on Dinefwr Castle, some twenty miles further up the Tywi.

'Standing on the summit of a high hill above the river', Dinefwr was a fortress of tremendous symbolic importance, for according to ancient tradition its owners were the rightful rulers of south Wales. Currently it belonged to Prince Rhys ap Gruffudd, but after his submission to Henry II in 1163, he had nearly lost it. The king sent a trusted Breton knight to report on the castle and its surroundings, equipping him with a Welsh guide under strict instructions to show him the easiest and most pleasant route. Instead, the cunning Welshman deliberately led him by the hardest, most roundabout tracks, stopping from time to time to munch handfuls of grass, which he declared was the usual food of the locals in times of shortage. When the exhausted envoy returned, therefore, he proclaimed in disgust that the Dinefwr area was totally inaccessible and uninhabitable, fit only for people who lived like wild animals — in short, it was simply not worth conquering. So Rhys was released from captivity, and Dinefwr remained Welsh. Much altered in later centuries, this most interesting fortress is at present undergoing a thorough repair and conservation.

Gerald's party, however, had no time to visit Dinefwr. Bound due west from Carmarthen, they were following the easy and well-trodden road (now the A40) through the St Clears district when they heard news of a terrible crime — a young Welshman, hurrying to meet them and take the cross, had been cruelly murdered by his enemies. His corpse still lay near the road, and Baldwin ordered it to be reverently covered with a cloak, saying a fervent prayer for the young man's soul before continuing to their destination. This was Whitland Abbey, now

Dinefwr Castle, traditionally the royal palace of the princes of south Wales, on its hill above the Tywi. Its round keep was built in the mid thirteenth century (Photograph by Roger Vlitos).

A thirteenth-century tile from Whitland Abbey, depicting the Lamb of God (By permission of the National Museum of Wales).

marked only by earthworks, but then famous as 'the old White House on the Taf', mother of all Welsh Cistercian monasteries. There, next morning, twelve archers from St Clears Castle confessed to the crime. Since their victim had not actually taken his vow, they avoided the execution and posthumous damnation prescribed for crusader-killers, and were allowed to expiate their offence by taking the cross themselves. It was not unusual, indeed, for criminals to be sentenced to go on crusade, though the practice can hardly have improved the quality of the Christian armies.

Then the travellers moved on westwards, following the medieval road which crossed the Eastern Cleddau river below Llawhaden Castle. As its dramatic ruins demonstrate, this stronghold of the bishops of St Davids was subsequently transformed into a luxurious fortified palace, but the wide ditch of the original 'ringwork' castle which Gerald knew still remains. A dozen years earlier, as a triumphant young reformer, he had watched the proud sheriff of Pembroke beaten there for defying him. (p. 12).

A much greater triumph lay in store for him at Haverfordwest, where the travellers arrived that night: Gerald never tired of talking about his achievement there, and accounts of it appear in several of his books. At first things looked black, for Gerald's kinsman, Sir Philip Mangonel, delivered a public warning that the mission was wasting its time — nobody in Haverfordwest would join the crusade, whatever Gerald or Baldwin might say. Though a huge crowd assembled next morning, indeed, so few of them responded to Baldwin's initial sermon that the archbishop was near despair when he handed over his preaching cross to Gerald. Then everything changed. Three times Gerald's preaching mounted to a crescendo, and each time his sermon was drowned by a throng clamouring for cloth crosses, almost trampling the archbishop in their wild enthusiasm. His entire audience, moreover, was moved to floods of tears — Baldwin later remarked that he had never seen so many tears in his life — and among

Haverfordwest, the scene of Gerald's miracle-working sermon in 1188. According to one of his stories, its castle above the River Cleddau was the prison of an enterprising bandit.

Llawhaden Castle, a fortified residence of the bishops of St Davids. In 1188 it was a powerful earth and timber 'ringwork' (see pp. 88-9) construction.

the most dedicated weepers was the once-sceptical Sir Philip, who took the cross with five or six other leading Pembrokeshire knights.

The really remarkable thing, however, was that Gerald achieved all this mainly by sheer force of personality. For he was preaching in Norman-French and Latin, and the vast majority of his audience understood not a word of either language. Yet the uncomprehending 'common folk' wept every bit as loudly as the French-speaking knights, and they responded with even greater eagerness, more than two hundred of them running forward all together to take the crusading vow. Many people therefore believed that something like a miracle had occurred, and Gerald did not contradict them. Nor was this the only wonder performed that day: for a turf from the place where Baldwin had preached, applied to the eyes of a blind old woman, immediately and miraculously restored her sight. Possibly the much-revered archbishop had more to do with the mission's success in Haverfordwest than Gerald cared to remember.

From here on, however, he had someone to assist his memory. For Gerald's book *Speculum Duorum* reveals that his twelve year old nephew William (his favourite brother Philip's son) joined the travellers at Haverfordwest, and rode with them throughout the remainder of their journey. Quite unruffled by leaving home for the first time, young William acted as a kind of human notebook, carefully observing events and memorizing conversations. Many years afterwards, as a grown-up knight, he could recount incidents which his uncle had long forgotten,

and we may perhaps owe some of the later additions to the *Journey through Wales* to the long memory of a sharp-eyed boy.

It may have been William's arrival, too, that launched Gerald on another round of tales, some tailor-made for a boy just leaving home. There were the children who became over-friendly with a bandit imprisoned in Haverfordwest Castle, who used to make them arrows: one day, however, he suddenly pulled them into his cell and threatened to chop them up, thus extorting a promise of his release. William would do much better to follow the example of Richard fitz Tancard, who had unexpectedly gained a great inheritance because of his boyish kindness to Gerald's favourite local holy man, Caradog of Rhos (p. 86).

The Haverford-Rhos area, with its robust, hard-working Flemish colonists — so adept at fortune-telling with boiled mutton-bones — bordered on the lordship of Pembroke. This was Gerald's homeland, and naturally he had a great deal to say about it. Its principal castle was Pembroke itself, today a magnificent stone fortress but protected only by weak turf and timber ramparts at the time when Gerald's grandfather cunningly defended it against the Welsh. After disguising his desperate lack of supplies by catapulting lumps of bacon at the besiegers, he wrote a confident letter declaring that he

Pembroke Castle's naturally strong site on a rocky promontory helped Gerald's grandfather to defend its earth and timber predecessor. Later additions, including the great round keep of about 1200, made it one of the mightiest fortresses in Wales.

would need no reinforcements for several months, and had it dropped as if by chance where he knew the enemy would find it. When they did, they abandoned the siege in despair and went home.

Somewhere within this same castle, Gerald remembered, a man had discovered a litter of weasel

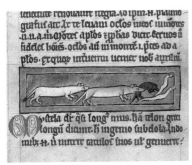

Weasels attacking rats, from a thirteenth-century bestiary (By permission of the British Library, Royal Ms. 12 C XIX, f.23v).

kittens, and carefully removed them. Thinking that he had killed them, the mother weasel was seen to revengefully spit poison into a jug of milk prepared for his baby son (everyone knew, of course, that weasels were deadly poisonous). But when her litter was returned unharmed, the grateful weasel immediately spilt the poisoned milk, so that the human child would likewise be saved. Much more valuable, however, were the local (peregrine?) falcons, the finest in all Henry II's broad realms. While the king had been hunting nearby in

Falconers hunting duck, from a thirteenth-century bestiary (By permission of the British Library, Harleian Ms. 4751, f.49).

1171, one of these had struck a much larger Norwegian hawk dead at his feet, and every year since he had sent for falcon-chicks from the Pembrokeshire sea cliffs to train in his royal mews.

Admittedly, the Pembroke region was also infested with an inconveniently large number of demons, poltergeists (pp. 84-5) and other supernatural nuisances. Yet it was undoubtedly the most beautiful part of all Wales, and the most attractive spot in it was undoubtedly Gerald's birthplace of Manorbier:

'There stands a castle [he enthused] with excellent towers and defences, set atop a coastal hill, which extends on its western side as far as the harbour. Towards the north, just beneath its walls, is a very good fishpond, notable both for its majestic appearance and the depth of its water. On the same side there is likewise a most beautiful orchard, enclosed between the pond and a wooded grove — itself remarkable both for rocky crags and tall hazel-trees. To the right-hand side of this fortified headland (that is to say between the castle and the church) a never-failing stream wanders down a valley, which is blown with sand by the power of the wind . . .'

The site of Manorbier Castle is still as beautiful as ever, and though much of the present building is somewhat later than Gerald's time, a small tower by the gate and the 'Norman hall' opposite may well have formed part of the buildings he knew and loved.

Only after a very long digression, indeed, could Gerald bear to turn from praising his homeland and continue his account of the travellers' progress. Leaving the scene of their triumph at Haverfordwest, they struck north-westwards through Camrose, and must have passed near the dramatic rocky outcrop of Roch — later crowned with a fairytale castle — before descending steeply to the sea and crossing Newgale Sands. Here, Gerald recalled, a tremendous storm sixteen years earlier had laid bare the remains of a great submerged forest (p. 81). Climbing onto dry land again, they then entered the stony and wind-tormented district of Pebydiog, or St David's Land, and that evening rode into the famous city of St Davids.

The idyllic site of Manorbier Castle, Gerald's birthplace. The ruined 'Norman Hall' in the centre of the picture may date from the time of his residence there (Photograph by Roger Vlitos).

St David and St Davids

by J. Wyn Evans

Remote, rocky and riverless; its soil too barren to sustain trees and pastures; exposed to winds and inclement weather; and caught between warring Flemings and hostile Welsh: such were the dismal attributes which Giraldus chose to highlight in his description of the St Davids at which he and Baldwin arrived in 1188. Doubtless, the 'good accommodation' with which the bishop, Peter de Leia, whom Giraldus — uncharacteristically — calls 'a most friendly and hospitable man', welcomed them, made up for these deficiencies. But can these be the words of a man who devoted most of his active life to promoting the status of St Davids; can this be the man who expended so much energy and ink in pursuing his claim to the bishopric of Menevia? Indeed yes; moreover, it is in the context of his efforts to secure — he would have said 'restore' — the metropolitan privileges of St Davids that Giraldus thus described the city and its environs in the *Itinerary*. He was comparing St Davids unfavourably with Caerleon as an ideal metropolitan centre since he erroneously believed that St Dyfrig and St David had removed the archbishopric from there. He tells us that they had deliberately chosen this remote site where David led a devout and saintly life. This account is, however, at variance with what Giraldus himself had written earlier of the patron saint's choice of *Vallis Rosina* as a site for his foundation.

The cathedral church and bishop's palace at St Davids from the south.

David, according to Giraldus, was the son of a prince of Ceredigion called Sant and 'a beautiful girl' called Nonnita whom he had met and violated in Pebydiog, the district in which St Davids lay. She gave birth to the saint in a spot marked in Giraldus' day by a church which may well be on the site of the present St Non's

The small chapel overlooking St Non's Bay is traditionally the site where Nonnita gave birth to St David.

Chapel. A well at Porthclais marked the place where David was baptised. He was brought up in *Vetus Rubus* (Hen Fynyw or Old Menevia). After his education under Paulinus, David and his companions settled in *Vallis Rosina*, after fending off the attacks of Boia and his wife. In the *Itinerary*, Giraldus provides a spectacularly false etymology for *Vallis Rosina*, suggesting that it would far better be called *Vallis Marmorea*, the marble valley, rather than the Vale of Roses, since rocks rather than roses characterized it in his day. The element *rosina*, however, precisely describes the location of the present cathedral since it is derived either from a Celtic word meaning 'marsh' or from one meaning 'promontory'. In his life of David, Giraldus relied heavily upon the Latin life written by Rhigyfarch, at the end of the eleventh century, some five centuries after the death of the saint. Like Rhigyfarch, he describes the pilgrimage to Jerusalem, when David was consecrated bishop by the patriarch and given gifts which could still be seen in Giraldus' day. Unlike Rhigyfarch, he does not describe the extreme asceticism which characterized David's monasticism, with the monks dressed in skins and hauling the ploughs on their own shoulders, but he includes one incident which Rhigyfarch does not: that of the 'Unfinished Gospel', a page of which had been written in angelic letters of gold. This relic, hidden

A contemporary image of St David by Sir Goscombe John, in Cardiff City Hall (By courtesy of Cardiff City Council).

from human sight since David's day, was still reverenced in Giraldus' time. Both Rhigyfarch and Giraldus are agreed in their account of the synod of Brefi, where David's eloquence in combating the Pelagian heresy was marked both by the descent of a dove and by the rising of the ground beneath his feet. Both authors also agree that it was as a result of the synod that David was made archbishop. David died on Tuesday 1 March, and was buried according to Rhigyfarch in the grounds of his own monastery. Giraldus does not specify the spot, but emphasizes the miracles associated with him.

By contrast, Giraldus' description of the St Davids he knew is of a place 'still the capital of Wales', but powerless and living on its past reputation — no longer 'our venerable and unchallenged mother — church'; no long 'the metropolitan city of an archbishop', which in the archdeacon's view it had once been. He spends an inordinate amount of space in the *Itinerary* tracing not only the successions of the 'archbishops' and bishops of Menevia but also how he believed the archiepiscopal *pallium* had been

The nave of St Davids Cathedral, which may not have been fully complete in 1188.

This rare survival of a fourteenth-century antiphoner, complete with music and illumination, represents the office for St David's Day. It may well come from south Wales (By courtesy of the National Library of Wales, Ms. 20541E, f.205v).

This modern reliquary, in the Holy Trinity Chapel at St Davids, is said to include bones of David himself (Photograph by Peter Humphries).

removed to Dol in Brittany in the time of St Samson. In his day *Vallis Rosina* was the site of a cathedral founded in honour of St Andrew the apostle. In *De Invectionibus*, written in 1216, in one of the numerous visions which Giraldus quotes as evidence for his predestined occupation of the see of Menevia, he refers to the 'old church of St Andrew' and 'the greater church' — presumably the present cathedral. The letter finds no place in the *Itinerary*, presumably because it had not been completed in 1188. The cathedral churchyard was bounded by the river Alun, a 'muddy and unproductive stream' in 1188, though it 'flowed with wine' in the time of his uncle Bishop David fitz Gerald. Across this stream lay the Llech Lafar over which Henry II had safely crossed in defiance of Welsh prophecy on Easter Monday 1172, when, after being met at the White Gate by the canons, he had entered the cathedral as a pilgrim. Giraldus reminded his readers that the cathedral precincts contained two prodigies: Pistyll Dewi, which had on occasion run with milk; and the jackdaws, whose kindly treatment at the hands of the local clergy had made them unafraid of anyone dressed in black.

The Journey through West Wales
St Davids to the Dovey

The present high altar in the presbytery at St Davids Cathedral, not yet built when Baldwin visited in 1188.

Beyond St Davids, and particularly beyond the Teifi, the nature of the country through which the mission journeyed changed once again. As it gradually grew more hilly, so it also became more Welsh — as indeed it still does today, when west Wales remains a stonghold of the Welsh language. In Gerald's time the division between south and west Wales was political as well as cultural. Whereas much of coastal south Wales was dominated by the Normans, with Welsh rulers maintaining a precarious independence on its fringes, in west Wales the roles were reversed:

help wondering exactly what the interpreter said to bring about this dramatic reversal, and whether his mistakes were perhaps deliberate.

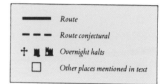

——	Route
– – –	Route conjectural
✝ ▦ ▩	Overnight halts
▢	Other places mentioned in text

St Davids to Strata Florida

beyond the few precarious Norman outposts on its southern edge, the land was firmly under Welsh control. In medieval terms, then, the travellers now passed out of the Normanized 'March of Wales' and into *pura Wallia* — 'absolute Wales' or 'Welsh Wales'. Here Prince Rhys ap

The arms traditionally attributed to Prince Rhys ap Gruffudd.

Gruffudd held sway without foreign rival, threatened only by the ambitions of his turbulent sons: and here, in own strong castle of Cardigan, he waited in state to greet the mission.

After saying a symbolic early morning Mass at the high altar of St Davids Cathedral, Archbishop Baldwin therefore hurried on towards Cardigan, entrusting Gerald with the task of preaching the crusade in St Davids city. This may have been a tactful compliment, but if so it misfired, for (as Gerald candidly admits in his autobiography, *De Rebus a se Gestis*) his Haverfordwest triumph was by no means repeated. While he preached in French or Latin to his largely Welsh-speaking audience, all went well, and many pressed forward eagerly to take the cross. But when an interpreter translated his sermon into Welsh ('in a much less orderly and acceptable fashion' than the original) these same would-be crusaders immediately changed their minds and withdrew their vows. One cannot

Doubtless in a furious temper, Gerald then set off to follow the archbishop. Journeying through the Cemais district — whose voracious toads had recently consumed an unlucky youth called Seisyll Longshanks (p. 83) — he skirted the northern flank of the Preseli Mountains and passed through Nevern. This was a shrine of legendary antiquity even in 1188. Its church, founded by St Brynach the Irishman during the sixth century, still displays some of the earliest Christian memorial stones in Wales, while in the churchyard stands a magnificent thirteen-foot Celtic cross — and a sinister yew tree, believed to shed blood.

The great pillar cross at Nevern, which must surely indicate the presence of a major pre-Conquest church nearby (Photograph by Heather James).

Hereabouts, Gerald related, a wealthy local man had thrice dreamt of a golden torc lying in St Brynach's Well: but when he searched there, he was fatally stung by a lurking adder. Nevern Castle, the complex and

The tree-grown outer motte of Nevern Castle.

impressive earthwork crowning the hill behind the church, was the scene of a less arbitrary working out of divine vengeance. Breaking a whole series of solemn oaths, Prince Rhys seized it from his Norman son-in-law and gave it to his son. Three years afterwards, however, another of his quarrelsome offspring captured him and imprisoned him in the very same place, a just punishment for his perfidy.

That evening Gerald caught up with Baldwin at St Dogmaels Abbey, whose ruins still survive in the little

The abbey of Tironian monks at St Dogmael's.

town above the Teifi. After a comfortable night there, they rode the short distance to the west end of Cardigan bridge, where they preached with great success to a huge crowd headed by Rhys and his sons. So great was the devotion they kindled, indeed, that the townsfolk decided to build a chapel on the exact spot where Baldwin had stood —

The Teifi bridge at Cardigan, where Baldwin and Gerald preached triumphant sermons.

perhaps they had heard of the miracle wrought by his footprint at Haverfordwest — while the hundred or so men recruited by Gerald more than made up for his reverse at St Davids. If only he had preached in Welsh, quipped Rhys's court jester, not one of the prince's followers would have been left unrecruited. One Cardigan matron, however, was less impressed: determined to prevent her husband taking the cross, she hauled him away bodily by his cloak and belt. Needless to say, she was mercilessly punished for depriving Christ of a would-be servant, for three nights later she accidentally smothered her beloved baby son as he lay in bed beside her. After that she raised no more objections to her husband's crusading, and sewed on his cloth cross with her own hands.

From now on, Rhys spared no trouble to honour the travellers. That night he entertained them splendidly, presumably in the (now almost vanished) 'old castle' a mile south-west of Cardigan, and next morning he set out with his two sons to escort them through his dominions, turning their journey into a royal progress. At first they took the road along the north side of the Teifi valley, leaving Crug Mawr with its magic burial-mound (p. 81) away to the left and cutting across the southward loop of the river guarded by Cilgerran Castle. Set on its towering rock above the Teifi gorge (and given its present twin-towered form in the following century) Cilgerran must surely be among the most spectacularly sited fortresses in all Wales. Once it had belonged to Gerald's family, and it was perhaps here that his notorious grandmother Nest was 'abducted' from under her furious husband's nose (pp. 7-8).

Cilgerran Castle dominates the Teifi gorge (Photograph by Roger Vlitos).

As the cavalcade continued westwards along Teifiside, Gerald launched into a description of the river's wonders. Unique in twelfth-century England and Wales for its surviving beavers (pp. 82-3), it was (and is) also famous for its abundance of fine salmon, which may well have been making their Spring spawning run over Cenarth Falls at the very time the travellers crossed the nearby bridge. There, by St Llawddog's church and mill, was,

'. . . a most productive fish pool, long ago hollowed into the top of a rock by the hands of the saint himself. The waters of Teifi, running down over this rock, plunge with a mighty roar into the depths below, while the salmon leap from the depths onto the top of the concave rock, a distance which equals the length of the longest spear'.

'Their leaps are quite amazing, and would seem miraculous if it was not the fish's nature to behave in this manner . . . They have a special way of leaping, which is this. When fish of this kind, naturally swimming against the current . . . meet a difficult obstacle, they bend their tail forward toward their mouth: sometimes, indeed, they actually grip their tail with their mouth, so as to make a better jump. Then they suddenly jerk themselves out of this circular form with great force (like a bent-over bough suddenly springing straight) and thus they leap long distances from the depths to the heights, to the wonder of all beholders'.

'They have a special way of leaping'. A salmon, from a thirteenth-century manuscript of Gerald's Topography of Ireland *(By permission of the British Library, Royal Ms. 13 B VIII).*

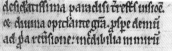

many took the cross. Then they pushed on again, travelling northwards through wilder and wilder country, until they skirted the great Red Bog of Tregaron and stopped for the night at Strata Florida Abbey, in its lonely setting against the backdrop of the windswept and almost uninhabited Cambrian Mountains.

The splendid and unusual west doorway of Strata Florida Abbey's church (Photograph by David Robinson).

Unlike the Normanized religious houses further south, Strata Florida was very much a Welsh monastery. Prince Rhys was its special patron, and only a few years before he had granted its sheep-farming Cistercian 'white monks' vast tracts of upland grazing, stretching clear across the mountains to Rhayader on the Wye. No doubt, therefore, he was anxious to show off the new church which was beginning to rise there in 1188: parts of its central and eastern sections (including the chapels afterwards paved with delightful medieval tiles) may already have been built, though the splendid west doorway belongs to a slightly later date. More Celtic than Norman in style, this doorway is a reminder of Strata Florida's continuing importance as a centre of medieval

Above: 'The waters of Teifi . . . plunge with a mighty roar into the depths below'. Cenarth Falls, with the successor of St Llawddog's mill.

Left: Modern coracle fishermen using a net on the Teifi.

Once the fish had leapt into St Llawddog's pool, they could be netted with relative ease, perhaps from coracles similar to those still to be seen on the Teifi. As Gerald warned in his *Description of Wales*, however, these tiny hide boats could easily be capsized by a flailing salmon, plunging the fisherman into the swirling rapids.

After a long day's ride by the river and over the Cardiganshire hills, the cavalcade reached Lampeter (or Pont Steffan as Gerald called it, using its Welsh name). Next morning no less than four sermons were preached there — by Baldwin, Gerald, and the Cistercian abbots of Whitland and Strata Florida, who had presumably joined the mission at Cardigan — and

Welsh culture, where Welsh national chronicles were compiled and Welsh princes were brought for burial. Rows of ancient tomb-slabs can still be seen east of the church, and hereabouts lie two of Rhys's sons.

Ornamental tiles at Strata Florida Abbey.

Grave-slabs of medieval Welsh princes and magnates, east of the abbey church at Strata Florida (Photograph by David Robinson).

As Gerald would later discover to his cost, however, Strata Florida's devotion to Welsh causes sometimes wavered. At the outset of his epic struggle for St Davids (pp. 24-5) he brought all his most valuable possessions here, including his 'treasure store of books, which he had zealously collected from his youth onwards': in this remote sanctuary, he believed, 'they would be safe from the power of the English, whatever might befall'. But when the issue began to be in doubt, the monks cold-shouldered him, exiling him to their public dormitory 'among the noise of the common folk' and denying him a guide through the surrounding wilderness. When he desperately needed cash for his final trip to Rome, moreover, they refused to accept his precious books as loan-security: instead, they insisted on

buying them at a knock-down price, leaving Gerald 'feeling as though his very bowels had been torn out'.

Whether the travellers preached at Strata Florida in 1188 is not clear, but they certainly did so very soon after they left the monastery the next day. Passing by a wood, they suddenly came upon Rhys's third son Cynwrig, leading his warband of lightly armed young companions. Every inch the noble savage, the tall, handsome, curly-haired Cynwrig was clad only in the traditional thin Welsh cloak and shirt, scorning to protect his bare legs and feet against briars and thistles. He was, cooed Gerald, 'a man adorned by nature, not by art, having a natural, not an artificial dignity'. Here, then, were Rhys and three of his sons, none of whom had yet taken the cross: the opportunity was too good to miss, and a sermon was preached to them on the spot. Their reaction was not encouraging. Cynwrig preferred dignity to action, while the eldest son Gruffudd ('a cunning twister', Gerald calls him elsewhere) was more anxious to get rid of his dashing brother Maelgwn than to leave Wales himself. After much argument, Maelgwn eventually agreed to accompany the mission to England, though he would not actually take the crusading vow.

After this halt, reports Gerald, 'we journeyed on through Llanddewi Brefi' — which seems a very odd route to take. From Strata Florida, the travellers were bound for Llanbadarn near Aberystwyth, some fifteen miles to the north-west by the usual medieval road: Llanddewi, however, is ten miles *south-west* of Strata Florida, so that they were now heading almost directly away from

their destination, adding nearly twenty miles to their day's journey and probably covering ground they had already traversed the day before. No explanation for this detour is given, and we can only speculate either that the more direct route to Llanbadarn was impassable, or else that the mission had some particular reason for visiting Llanddewi, but had been in too much of a hurry to do so on the previous day.

Strata Florida to Nefyn

——	Route
– – –	Route conjectural
✝ 🏰 🏰	Overnight halts
☐	Other places mentioned in text

Nefyn

Castell Aber Ia

Carn Fadryn

Llanfair

Bardsey Island

River Mawddach

Cymmer Abbey

N

0   10 miles

River Dysnni

River Dovey

Tywyn

✝ Llanbadarn Fawr

Strata Florida ✝

☐ Llanddewi Brefi

Certainly Llanddewi Brefi was a shrine of great significance for the Welsh Church. Many centuries earlier, St David himself had preached there to a huge crowd from all over Wales, striving to refute the Pelagian heresy which then threatened the unity of Christendom. At first he was unable to make himself heard, but then the earth beneath his feet miraculously swelled up into a hillock, lifting him high above the throng. As a result, Gerald claimed, the saint was immediately and unanimously hailed as archbishop of all Wales — a controversial claim, since his successors at St Davids were now mere bishops, subject to the rule of Canterbury. Doubtless, therefore, the visit prompted some lively disputes among the travellers.

Llanddewi's fine church still stands on the saint's miraculous hillock above the Brefi stream, and though much rebuilt since the mission's visit, it preserves many reminders of its former greatness. Beneath its massive central tower, for example, is an ancient monolith known as St David's Staff, while in its exterior north-west wall is set a fragment of the 'David Stone', recording the killing of a man who dared to plunder the saint's sanctuary.

At this point the cavalcade turned north again, most probably following the Roman road called Sarn Helen (now the B4578/A485) for much of the distance to Llanbadarn Fawr — 'the great church of St Padarn', near which the town of Aberystwyth grew up in later centuries. Here they stayed overnight, and in the morning recruited many crusaders, but this success did nothing to mitigate Gerald's vehement disapproval of the place. What he found there (on the site of the present vast and austere thirteenth-century church) was a *clas*, or Welsh religious community of married canons, whose property passed from priestly father to priestly son. Such communities originated during the earliest years of Welsh Christianity, and Llanbadarn in

St David's church at Llanddewi Brefi, on the saint's miraculously-raised hillock.

particular had once been famous for its long tradition of holiness and learning. In recent decades, however, it had passed through many troubles. First the Norman invaders had expelled its Welsh canons, replacing them with Anglo-Norman monks from St Peter's at Gloucester (an excellent move, thought Gerald, especially since this was his old school). Then the Welsh princes, reconquering the region, had reinstated the native canons: but Llanbadarn's glory had departed, and by 1188 it was a community in decline, confirming all Gerald's darkest suspicions about the decadence of the Celtic Church.

Unlike the monasteries he knew, with their strictly celibate monks and elected abbots, Llanbadarn was run as a family concern. To make matters worse, its so-called abbot was not even a cleric, but 'a wicked old layman called Ednywain ap Gwaethfoed', who enjoyed the community's revenues while his priestly sons officiated at its altars. This state of affairs, Gerald declared, was a scandal unparalleled anywhere

in the civilized world: a much-travelled foreign tourist had been unutterably shocked to see the abbot processing into the church carrying a long spear, surrounded by an armed bodyguard. Why no-one had ever complained about it was beyond Gerald's comprehension. Perhaps he expected Baldwin to take action, but nothing was done, and the outraged reformer relapsed into impotent mutterings. Doubtless the archbishop had more sense than to interfere with local customs, especially while Prince Rhys was looking on.

Rhys's stay with the mission, however, was drawing to a close, and so was that of Bishop Peter. For less than ten miles north of Llanbadarn lay the Dovey estuary, the traditional dividing line between north and south Wales and the boundary both of Rhys's territory and the diocese of St Davids. There prince and bishop turned for home, leaving the much-reduced band of travellers to cross the river by boat and begin the last leg of their journey through Wales.

Gerald and the Princes of Wales

by R. R. Davies

Gerald of Wales was very well placed to comment on the princes of Wales of his day, for he knew most of them personally if not intimately and was related to a fair number of them. Gerald, it is true, was a great boaster and an inveterate name-dropper, but when he remarked that he was 'related by blood to almost all the princes and great men of Wales' his claim was not an idle one. He was first cousin once removed of the most powerful Welsh ruler of his day, Lord Rhys of Deheubarth (d. 1197), and could easily expound a relationship, albeit often by marriage, with most of the other native dynasties of north and south Wales. Nor were these men merely names on a family tree (see genealogical table, p. 60). Gerald was well aquainted with most of them and made the most of the family links when it suited him — joining Lord Rhys at dinner in the bishop of Hereford's house and visiting him as an envoy at Llandovery, basking in the hospitality of the princes of Gwynedd at Rhuddlan and Aberconwy, persuading one of the chieftains of mid-Wales to help him get the better of the bishop of St Asaph in an ecclesiastical quarrel, and borrowing money from another kinsman, this time a Welsh prince of Glamorgan, when he was short of cash in France.

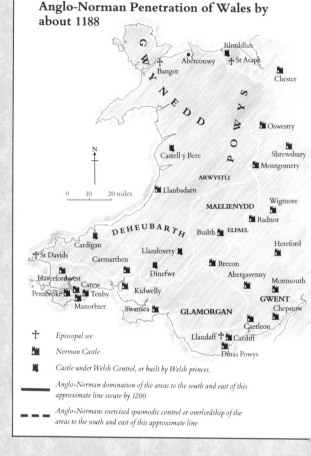

Anglo-Norman Penetration of Wales by about 1188

† Episcopal see

🏰 Norman Castle

🏰 Castle under Welsh Control, or built by Welsh princes.

——— Anglo-Norman domination of the areas to the south and east of this approximate line secure by 1200

- - - Anglo-Normans exercised spasmodic control or overlordship of the areas to the south and east of this approximate line

This fourteenth-century effigy in St Davids Cathedral is generally believed to be a memorial to the Lord Rhys. The most powerful Welsh ruler of Gerald's day, he died in 1197.

Gerald, in short, knew the world of Welsh politics from the inside. He had the further advantage that he was writing about Wales at a particularly interesting period. By the second half of the twelfth century the Anglo-Norman advance into Wales — which had once looked overwhelming and irresistible — had been halted and indeed reversed in many areas. The March of Wales, as the area under Norman control was called, was now confined to a fairly narrow band of fertile and low-lying land along the south coast and eastern borders of Wales and a secondary zone beyond this band where Anglo-Norman control was much more tentative and insecure. The remainder of Wales — now sometimes referred to as 'pure Wales' — was ruled by native Welsh dynasties. The three major Welsh principalities were Gwynedd in the north-west, Powys in the north-east and central Wales, and Deheubarth in the south-west; but smaller Welsh principalities also survived in the upland districts of eastern Wales (especially Arwystli, Maelienydd and Elfael), Gwent and Glamorgan. An uneasy equilibrium of power had been established between these native Welsh dynasties on the one hand and the Anglo-Norman barons and kings on the other. The blood of both parties, Welsh and Norman, ran in Gerald's veins, so he was well placed to write with sympathy and insight about both.

What struck him above all about Welsh princes and nobles was their militarism. They delighted in arms and in war; they went about in armed retinues and counted military glory and a heroic death as the greatest virtues. It was their boundless military

'A man of more fluent speech than his fellow princes and conspicuous for the good governance of his land'. Such was Gerald's character sketch of Owain Cyfeiliog, prince of southern Powys (d. 1198). But there was another side to Owain's character: he was a warrior prince in the heroic mould and a very talented poet. His poem to 'The Long Blue Drinking Horn' is one of the most evocative poems in medieval Welsh.

The Red Book of Hergest is the single most valuable volume of Welsh medieval literature. Written in the last quarter of the fourteenth century, it contains Owain Cyfeiliog's poem, 'The Long Blue Drinking Horn' (By courtesy of the Principal and Fellows, Jesus College, Oxford).

'A man of distinguished wisdom and moderation'. This was Gerald's lavish tribute to Owain 'the Great', prince of Gwynedd (d. 1170). But Gerald thoroughly disapproved of Owain's marriage to a close relative — a common Welsh custom in Gerald's opinion — and recommended that his body should be removed from its tomb in Bangor Cathedral as soon as possible as a punishment for his refusal to give up his wife as the church demanded (see illustration of inscribed stone p. 61).

appetite, their high degree of skill in guerrilla warfare and their 'love of liberty' (in Gerald's words) which had enabled them to withstand the Normans and eventually to wear them down. Gerald captured their almost desperate heroism in his memorable accounts of the dare-devil attacks on the Norman castles of Abergavenny and Cardiff (see pp. 34, 39). He had a sneaking admiration for the remarkable resilience they showed in defeat and for their capacity to make a comeback, even when that recovery was at the expense of Gerald's own family. No one typified these Welsh virtues to better effect than the Lord Rhys: starting with no more than a tiny foothold in the uplands beyond the Tywi valley he had, through

Castell Aber Iâ, near Portmeirion, is the probable site of Deudraeth Castle, mentioned by Gerald in 1188 as one of the two stone castle newly erected by Welsh princes (see p. 63). The present stone tower is a twentieth-century folly (Photograph by Richard Avent).

Castell y Bere, Gwynedd, built largely by Llywelyn the Great in the years after 1221.

military skill and the force of his personality, rebuilt the Welsh principality of Deheubarth. His success, like that of the Welsh in general, was in part to be explained by his capacity to learn lessons from the Normans, especially in the art of cavalry warfare and castle building. The Welsh princes rebuilt and extended Norman castles which they captured (as the Lord Rhys did at Cardigan and Llandovery) and also constructed castles of their own (such as Dinefwr in the Tywi valley or Castell y Bere).

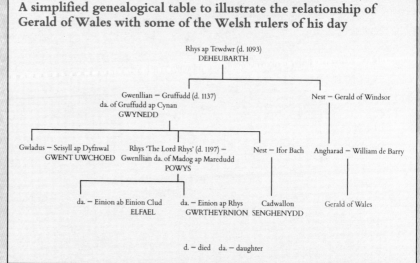

A simplified genealogical table to illustrate the relationship of Gerald of Wales with some of the Welsh rulers of his day

Rhys ap Tewdwr (d. 1093)
DEHEUBARTH

Gwenllian — Gruffudd (d. 1137)
da. of Gruffudd ap Cynan
GWYNEDD

Nest — Gerald of Windsor

Gwladus — Seisyll ap Dyfnwal
GWENT UWCHOED

Rhys 'The Lord Rhys' (d. 1197) —
Gwenllian da. of Madog ap Maredudd
POWYS

Nest — Ifor Bach

Angharad — William de Barry

da. — Einion ab Einion Clud
ELFAEL

da. — Einion ap Rhys
GWRTHEYRNION

Cadwallon
SENGHENYDD

Gerald of Wales

d. — died   da. — daughter

In spite of their remarkable resilience and their capacity to learn from their enemies, the Welsh had one fatal shortcoming — 'they obstinately and proudly refuse to submit to one ruler', as Gerald put it. Occasionally, a powerful prince such as Lord Rhys or, after his death, Llywelyn the Great of Gwynedd (d. 1240) might manage to secure a supremacy over some or all of the other native princes; but such a supremacy rarely outlived the life of one prince and was in any case never more than the masterful chairmanship of a federation of principalities. Furthermore, each princely dynasty was often bitterly divided within itself by feuds between competing relatives, each of whom believed that by Welsh custom he had the right to a share of the inheritance. Such feuds frequently ended in appalling bloodbaths and provided ideal opportunities for the

The great seal [cast], 1205-6, of Llywelyn the Great of Gwynedd (By permission of the National Museum of Wales).

Following the death of Llywelyn the Great in 1240, his sons Dafydd and Gruffudd were soon engaged in power-struggles within Gwynedd. Gruffudd was eventually held in royal custody at the Tower of London. Impatient for freedom, in 1244 he fell to his death in an attempt to escape. This depiction of the event is by the contemporary chronicler Matthew Paris (By permission of the British Library, Royal Ms. 14 C VII, f.136).

Dolwyddelan in Gwynedd, one of the castles of Llywelyn the Great. Nearby, are the slight remains of an earlier Welsh castle on a natural rocky hillock.

This inscribed stone at Llanfihangel y Traethau is a memorial to 'Wleder', who first built the church there 'in the time of King Owain'. This probably refers to Owain Gwynedd, prince of Gwynedd, who died in 1170 (By courtesy of the National Monuments Record, Wales).

king of England to intervene in Welsh politics and to further destabilize the Welsh principalities. Gerald had witnessed the way that Gwynedd was dismembered by such divisions after the death of Owain Gwynedd in 1170 and Deheubarth after Lord Rhys's death in 1197. It is little wonder that he came to believe that the only hope for the Welsh was to unite behind 'one prince and he a good one'. The survival of Wales as an independent country would depend on how far it recognized Gerald's diagnosis of its political malaise and adopted his cure for it.

The Journey through North Wales

Across the Dovey rose the mountains of Merioneth, the southernmost district of Gwynedd and

'. . . the wildest and most terrifying region in all Wales. For its mountains are very high and inaccessible, with crags as sharply pointed as the defences of a fortress. Nor are these mountains widely spaced out, but all jumbled so closely together that shepherds can exchange comments or abuse from neighbouring peaks: if they ever decided to meet face to face, however, a whole day's journey would scarcely bring them together'.

Beyond Merioneth the mountain ranges continued northwards towards Anglesey and north-eastwards to the distant Vale of Clwyd, making Gwynedd the poorest and most sparsely-populated of the Welsh principalities. But they also turned its interior into a natural stronghold, while the many hazardous estuaries which cut into the coast road round its fringes rendered it difficult even to attack. In Gerald's time, indeed, it was a region completely free from the threat of Norman domination, and it would remain the heartland of Welsh independence for almost another century. Only by bringing to bear the entire resources of England would Edwards I eventually conquer it, and only by ringing its mountains with the most costly and impressive series of castles in medieval Europe — Harlech, Caernarfon, Conwy and the rest — could he complete its subjugation.

In this bastion of 'pure Wales', Gerald the Pembrokeshire Marcher was something of an outsider. He did not know the country well, and he never mentions preaching there: probably he never did so, for there were no Norman settlers to understand his French, and comparatively few clerics to appreciate his Latin. Though he was distantly related to its princes, moreover, he was not on such easy terms with them as he was with Rhys ap Gruffudd. For the time being, indeed, Gwynedd possessed no equivalent of Prince Rhys, no single undisputed ruler to smooth the mission's progress. The great Owain Gwynedd had been such a man, but he was now dead, and his principality was uneasily divided among his sons and grandsons, each carefully watching for an opportunity to seize the others' inheritance.

Thus the mission entered Gwynedd unheralded and ungreeted, riding northward along the sandy coastline to spend the night at Tywyn, whose 'lofty church of St Cadfan by the blue sea' was famous as 'the glory of Merioneth'. The severely plain twelfth-century nave which Gerald saw there still survives, and there, too, is the ancient 'Cadfan stone', carved with what may be the earliest inscription in the Welsh language. Early next morning, however, Gruffudd ap Cynan — lord of Merioneth and the great Owain's grandson — galloped into Tywyn, humbly and devoutly begging Baldwin's pardon for failing to meet them earlier. His mortification was doubtless sincere, for Gruffudd was a notably pious prince. Ten years later, he and his brother Maredudd would found the modest little Cistercian abbey of Cymer, whose ruins stand in a beautiful setting near Dolgellau, by the confluence (Welsh: 'cymer') of the rivers Mawddach and Wynion. It was probably hereabouts that Gerald and Baldwin crossed the two rivers by

The mountains of Merioneth, seen across the Dovey estuary.

The thirteenth-century church of Cymmer Abbey, from the south (Photograph by David Robinson).

Castell Aber Îa near Portmeirion, which once guarded the spit of land between the two great tide-covered sands of Traeth Mawr and Traeth Bychan. If so, Gerald must have passed close by it, for the travellers traversed these formidable obstacles on their way to the Lleyn peninsula — where the second new fortress, Carn Fadryn, stood within the defences of an ancient hillfort above the hamlet of Dinas.

Off the western tip of Lleyn, wrote Gerald, lay the holy isle of Bardsey, home of the exceptionally pious hermit-monks called Coelibes

boat, while the impetuous Maelgwn ap Rhys (the reluctant crusader of Strata Florida) found a more direct though more hazardous route across the Mawddach estuary, which he forded near the sea.

Skirting the dark and rugged Rhinog Mountains, the cavalcade then continued northwards along the coast road to the little village of Llanfair in Ardudwy, where they stayed the night. Next day they preached their first sermon in Gwynedd from a nearby bridge, where Gruffudd's younger brother, Prince Maredudd, had assembled the men of the region to await them. Many took the cross, including 'a very fine young man of Maredudd's warband, one of his closest friends'. As the crusader symbol was about to be sewn to this man's cloak, the tender-hearted prince noticed how thin and threadbare it was: bursting into floods of tears, he immediately threw his own much better cloak round his friend's shoulders.

This incident probably took place near Harlech, whose rock was as yet uncrowned by Edward I's magnificent fortress. In 1188, however, two new castles had recently been constructed in the region, and Gerald emphasized the remarkable facts that they were built in stone, and by Welsh princes: hitherto (where they had built castles at all) the native rulers seem to have made do with old-fashioned earth-and-timber strongholds, so these new fortresses may have been among the very earliest stone castles in Gwynedd. The first, Deudraeth (or 'two sands') was most probably

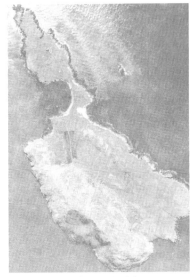

A vertical aerial view of Bardsey, island of saints.

A 'Culdee' monk inscribing a manuscript, from a twelfth-century copy of Gerald's Topography of Ireland (By courtesy of the National Library of Ireland, Ms. 700).

('celibates') or Culdees (from the Irish 'servants of God'). Whether he ever visited their inaccessible sea-girt rock is doubtful, but he knew all about it by reputation, for it was one of the most renowned shrines in Wales. In this island of the blessed, disease was so rare that scarcely anyone died except of extreme old age, and in its hallowed soil lay the bodies of myriad saints.

The mission's route, however, took them well clear of both Carn Fadryn and Bardsey. Emerging from the great sands somewhere near the site of later Criccieth Castle, they struck across Lleyn for Nefyn on the north coast of the peninsula, the chief town and princely court of the region. There Gerald made a most exciting discovery — nothing less than the fabled book of the prophecies of Merlin Silvester, which he had long but vainly sought in all the remotest corners of Wales. In his *Conquest of Ireland*, he provides more details of his sensational find. The book, he claimed, had been kept hidden at Nefyn since time immemorial, and was regarded with superstitious awe by the inhabitants: before they agreed to hand it over, he had to back up his persuasions with a hefty bribe. It was, moreover, written in the 'ancient British language', and Gerald had no doubt that it was genuine. Yet he never kept his promise to publish it in full, and in later editions of the *Conquest* he carefully suppressed all extracts from it, while in the final version of the *Journey through Wales* he even altered his account of its discovery, changing 'he found it' to 'he is said to have found it'. Did Gerald eventually come to believe, therefore, that his great discovery was a fake? Or did he invent the whole incident, but afterwards suffer from a troubled conscience? All the same, Nefyn was just the place where such a volume might have survived, for a persistent tradition linked it with King Arthur and his court. Nearly a century later, the legend-loving Edward I would make a point of

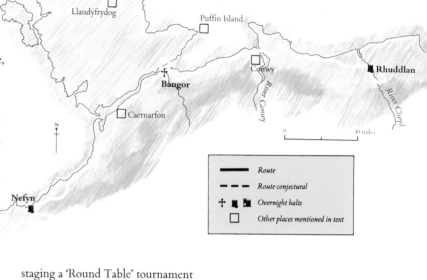

Nefyn to Rhuddlan

staging a 'Round Table' tournament there, thus proclaiming himself the heir of 'the once and future king' of all Britain.

The Welsh castle of Criccieth was taken by King Edward I in 1283, and was subsequently modified.

The mission, of course, had not come to Nefyn to search for dubious prophecies. They had arrived there on the eve of Palm Sunday, and on the feast day itself Baldwin preached the crusade, persuading many to take the cross. Then they hurried on towards distant Bangor, one of the longest and most exhausting day's journeys of the entire expedition. After threading their way through the mountains of northern Lleyn, passing close to the great hillfort of Tre'r Ceiri on the

On the road from Caernarfon to Bangor, fatigue began to take its toll — after all, they had already covered twenty miles that day, and had been on their travels for well over a month — and Gerald provides us with an extraordinarily vivid snapshot of the flagging mission, buoyed up by the

old archbishop's never-failing cheerfulness. 'Our route led us to a valley, whose downward slope was just as steep and rugged as the climb

Nant y Garth, supposedly the site of the mission's exhausted halt.

The stone-built ramparts and hut-circles of Tre'r Ceiri hillfort (Copyright: Cambridge University Collection).

summit of Yr Eifl, they rode along the coastal plain of Arfon ('the country opposite Môn', 'the land facing Anglesey') and through Caernarfon — 'Y Gaer yn Arfon', the stronghold in Arfon, meaning the Roman fortress of *Segontium,* whose excavated remains can still be seen south-east of the town. In 1188, however, this had been superseded by a Norman-built castle on the shores of the Menai Strait: and there, almost a hundred years afterwards, Edward I would raise his own Caernarfon Castle, most famous of all his Welsh fortresses.

Caernarfon, with the site of Segontium Roman fort in the foreground, and Edward I's great castle in the distance.

out of it'. [This valley has been identified, without much evidence, as Nant y Garth, near Port Dinorwic]:

'So we all dismounted from our horses and trudged on afoot, agreeing that we were already experiencing, or at least rehearsing, some of the hardships of our future pilgrimage to Jerusalem. By the time we had crossed the ravine and toiled up the far side, everyone was tired out, and the archbishop was glad to sit down on an oak tree uprooted by the wind, for he needed to rest and get his breath back. Then, relaxing into a jollity very praiseworthy in a man of his great dignity, he said to those standing by, "Now, which of you in all this company can delight our weary ears by whistling a tune" — this, of course, being very difficult for people exhausted by their travels. He himself, he insisted, could do so if he really wanted to'.

'At that moment a little bird was heard to whistle very sweetly in a neighbouring wood. Some said it was a woodpecker, others, more correctly, insisted it was an "aureolus" . . . this bird is very conspicuous for its golden-yellow colour, and sometimes it whistles sweetly instead of singing'.

[It was probably a golden oriole, which does indeed whistle, and can easily be mistaken for a green woodpecker, which does not].

'Someone then remarked that the nightingale was never seen in these parts, and the archbishop, smiling quietly but meaningfully, quipped. "The nightingale is a well-advised bird, if it never comes near Wales. We, on the other hand, must be fools, for we have not only come into Wales, but also travelled right round it!"'

That night the way-worn travellers reached Bangor, then as now the cathedral city of Gwynedd: the present cathedral church there is the successor of the one which Gerald knew, and which was fated to be destroyed two decades afterwards by King John's marauding mercenaries. Its Welsh Bishop Gwion looked after the mission well, standing dutifully by his high altar while Baldwin celebrated a symbolic Mass there next morning. Despite the urgings of the

Bangor Cathedral, the successor of Bishop Gwion's church.

archbishop and others, however, he steadfastly resisted joining the crusade, and eventually had to be coerced into taking the cross — whereupon his faithful flock set up a deafening chorus of wailings, moans and lamentations.

Immediately after this somewhat disconcerting experience, the travellers took ship across the narrow Menai Strait to Anglesey, where Prince Rhodri ab Owain had mustered the local inhabitants in a natural rocky amphitheatre near the sea (according to tradition, this was at a place called Cerrig y Borth, not far from the Menai suspension bridge). There, three sermons were preached, one by Baldwin and two in Welsh by Archdeacon Alexander the interpreter and Abbot Seisyll of Strata Florida, so that many of the 'ordinary folk' were recruited. But the aristocratic young men of Rhodri's household remained as immovable as the rock they sat on: attempting to persuade them to take the cross, claimed Gerald, was like trying to get honey from a stone, or oil from a boulder. As we might have expected, they were duly punished for their obduracy. Within the regulation three days, most of them had been slain by bandits, and the chastened survivors cut the cross they had scorned into their own flesh. Their master Prince Rhodri likewise paid the price of obstinacy: having ignored

Baldwin's advice to cast off his incestuous mistress, he was soon afterwards driven out of Anglesey by his nephews, Maredudd and Gruffudd of Merioneth.

Gerald can have spent only a few hours on Anglesey in 1188, but he picked up a great deal of information to pass on to his readers. Though it looked as barren and arid as the land around St Davids, it was really very fertile: indeed, it was renowned as 'Môn Mam Cymru' ('Anglesey, Mother of Wales') because it was capable of growing enough corn to feed the whole nation. Among its many wonders was a miraculous thigh-shaped stone, which not only returned home of its own accord whenever it was removed, but also served local couples as a useful contraceptive (p. 81). Much holier and more powerfully protected was the church of St Tyfrydog, at Llandyfrydog near Llanerchymedd. The Norman Earl Hugh of Shrewsbury had been impious enough to kennel his hounds there, and a month later he was killed while galloping into the surf to attack an incoming Viking fleet. Only his eyes were left unprotected by his complete suit of mail, yet that was exactly where an arrow fired by the Norse King Magnus Barelegs struck him, penetrating straight into his brain. 'Now let him leap up, if he can', sneered Magnus from the prow of his ship.

After this dreadful working out of St Tyfrydog's curse, the Normans might have been expected to leave his church well alone. But as Gerald knew from his own family history, two of his half-uncles had led a force to plunder it in 1157, with equally dire results. For Henry fitz Henry (grandmother Nest's son by Henry I) was soon afterwards stuck full of spears by the vengeful islanders, while Robert fitz Stephen (her son by another lover) was badly wounded in the rout, and escaped only with difficulty.

Their recruiting on Anglesey completed, the travellers retired to spend a second night in Bangor, where someone proudly showed them the tomb of the great Prince Owain Gwynedd in the cathedral.

One of the wonders of Anglesey (see p. 81). The prehistoric passage grave of Bryn Celli Ddu – 'the mound of the dark grove' – raised within a circular henge.

(see p. 81)

The arms traditionally attributed to Owain Gwynedd

The sight, however, did not please them, for Owain had died excommunicate, and excommunicated by no less an authority than the sainted Archbishop Thomas Becket. So he had no business to be lying in hallowed ground, and poor Bishop Gwion was odered to eject his corpse as soon as possible — an action which, to say the least, was likely to provoke local controversy. Then, leaving the much-tried bishop with his problem (he is said to have solved it by tunnelling secretly into the tomb) they set out next morning on the coast road to Conwy.

As they rode out of Bangor, Priestholm (also known as Puffin Island and Ynys Seiriol, recalling its connection with Seiriol's surviving Penmon Priory in Anglesey) was clearly visible across the sea to the north. There, Gerald reported, lived another community of pious hermit-monks like those of Bardsey. No women were ever allowed onto the island, but it was infested with 'tiny little mice' — most probably they were voles — and if the hermits fell to quarrelling among themselves, these diminutive servants of God brought them to their senses by eating up all their provisions.

Further east (presumably between Llanfairfechan and Penmaenmawr) the road skirted the sea's edge, while the rocky cliffs of the Carneddau Mountains rose up on the landward side, reminding Gerald of the manifold wonders of Snowdonia. His thoughts turned first to Dinas Emrys, the ancient and legend-haunted hillfort near Beddgelert, where Merlin Emrys — the demon-fathered Merlin of Carmarthen — had prophesied to King Vortigern, revealing the pair of dragons which lived in the pool beneath it: a pool, incidentally, which can still be seen there. This Merlin's prophecies, however, were nothing like so valuable as those of Merlin Silvester, which Gerald claimed to be carrying among his baggage.

Stretching from Merioneth to the mouth of the Conwy, the cloud-capped mountains of Snowdonia were known in Welsh as 'Eryri', 'the haunt of eagles'. Appropriately, a fabulous eagle was said to live there, perching on a certain stone every Thursday because it thought that a battle would be fought nearby on that day of the week: apparently it had been awaiting its prey for centuries, for it had almost worn a hole through the stone with its beak. No less remarkable were two mountain lakes,

one containing only one-eyed fish and the other a wind-blown floating island, which sometimes bore away sheep grazing upon it. Indeed, Snowdonia was renowned for its vast and inexhaustible mountain pastures: 'just as Anglesey could provide all the inhabitants of Wales with corn', ran the old proverb, 'so Eryri could supply grazing for all the herds of Wales put together'.

Penmon Priory in Anglesey once belonged to the hermit-monks of Priestholm.

The legend-haunted hillfort of Dinas Emrys, in Snowdonia (Photograph by Peter Humphries).

The young Merlin Emrys and Vortigern at Dinas Emrys (see pp. 36-7). Below them are the pool dwelling dragons of Merlin's prophecy. From a thirteenth-century manuscript (By permission of the British Library, Cotton Claudius Ms. B VII, f.224).

Snowdonia, the grazing-ground and innermost natural stronghold of Gwynedd.

Eagles flying towards the sun. From a thirteenth-century bestiary (By permission of the British Library, Royal Ms. 2 C XIX, f.38).

Leaving the mountains behind them, the travellers next crossed the Conwy estuary by boat, to land on the further shore somewhere near Deganwy Castle. If Anglesey was the granary of Gwynedd, and Snowdonia its grazing-ground and innermost natural stronghold, the broad Conwy river was its most vital line of defence, cutting across the coast road into the principality and blocking

the invasion route from England. Control of its crossings was thus the key to north Wales, and a century later Edward I would build his great castle and fortress-town of Conwy on the west bank of the river. [Here Edward meant to establish the capital of conquered Gwynedd, so his mighty castle was equipped as a royal palace, while outside its gates he founded a new town for immigrant English settlers, enclosing it with a three quarter mile long circuit of walls, towers and gatehouses.]

An aerial view of King Edward I's castle and town walls at Conwy, the most impressive complex of surviving medieval fortifications in Britain.

In Gerald's time, however, Welsh-held Deganwy still dominated the estuary, and the future site of Edward's stronghold was occupied by the Cistercian monastery of Aberconwy, whose much-rebuilt church is now the parish church of Conwy town. Six years after the mission passed, the simmering feud between the rival princes of Gwynedd came to a head in a bloody battle hereabouts, when Llywelyn ab Iorwerth (though scarcely more than a boy) defeated his powerful uncle,

A sculptured head from Deganwy, said to represent Prince Llywelyn ab Iorwerth (By permission of the National Museum of Wales).

Dafydd ab Owain Gwynedd. Gerald could not resist moralizing on these events in later editions of his book, attributing Llywelyn's success to the fact that he was legitimate, whereas Dafydd (at least in Gerald's view) was a bastard, and thus plainly in disfavour with Heaven. His enthusiasm for Llywelyn also made good sense politically, for the victor became Llywelyn the Great, mightiest of the medieval rulers of Gwynedd and one of Gerald's firmest supporters in his struggle for St Davids (pp. 24-5).

But for the time being Prince Dafydd remained apparently secure in his rule over eastern Gwynedd. He it was who welcomed the travellers at the end of their long day's ride from

Bangor, hospitably urging them to stay in his castle at Rhuddlan and entertaining them royally there. The impressive remains of this castle — an enormous sixty foot high mound, now known as Twthill — can still be seen a few hundred yards from Edward I's later stone castle. When Gerald and Baldwin visited it, the mound was probably crowned by a wooden keep, and a bailey surrounded by palisades and ditches extended below its northern flank. Beyond the bailey, moreover, yet another set of earth and timber fortifications defended the borough established beneath the castle's shadow: while to the south and east a steep drop to the marshy river Clwyd provided natural protection for both town and castle.

A suggested reconstruction of the motte and bailey castle at Rhuddlan as it may have appeared about 1188 (Illustration by John Banbury).

King Edward I's Castle at Rhuddlan.

Guarding the crossing of the Clwyd, Gwynedd's forward line of defence against invasion, Rhuddlan had been a storm centre of border wars for centuries. The Anglo-Saxon armies of King Offa of Mercia (whose famous dyke can still be traced a few miles to the east) and later of King Harold Godwinson had fought battles against the Welsh there, and there the Norman freebooter Robert 'of Rhuddlan' founded the castle and borough as his base for operations against north Wales. As such, the fortress remained a thorn in the side of the native princes until two decades before the mission's visit, when a grand alliance of Owain Gwynedd and Rhys ap Gruffudd had wrested it from the invader after an epic three-month siege.

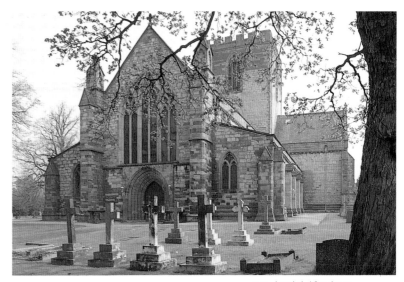

St Asaph Cathedral from the east.

Rhuddlan to Shrewsbury

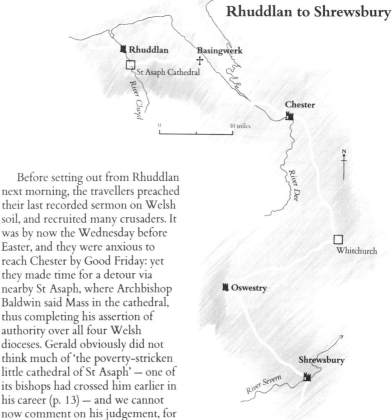

Before setting out from Rhuddlan next morning, the travellers preached their last recorded sermon on Welsh soil, and recruited many crusaders. It was by now the Wednesday before Easter, and they were anxious to reach Chester by Good Friday: yet they made time for a detour via nearby St Asaph, where Archbishop Baldwin said Mass in the cathedral, thus completing his assertion of authority over all four Welsh dioceses. Gerald obviously did not think much of 'the poverty-stricken little cathedral of St Asaph' — one of its bishops had crossed him earlier in his career (p. 13) — and we cannot now comment on his judgement, for the church he knew was totally destroyed during subsequent border upheavals. Its successor, an attractive though heavily restored building of the later Middle Ages, remains much the smallest of Welsh pre-Reformation cathedrals.

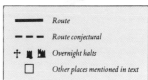

——	Route
– – –	Route conjectural
✝ ♜ ♜♜	Overnight halts
☐	Other places mentioned in text

Then the mission pressed on eastwards through the long-disputed border province of Tegeingl, between the Clwyd and the Dee. Gerald noted its rich veins of silver, exploited since Roman times and still being mined in 1188, and mentions a local spring whose waters unaccountably rose and sank several times a day. Equally unaccountably, he says nothing about the much more famous holy well of St Winefred, even then renowned for its miraculous curative powers and still a magnet for hopeful pilgrims today, nearly five centuries after Lady Margaret Beaufort built the splendid late medieval shrine-chapel which encases it (p. 87). Yet he must have passed very close to its site, for the travellers spent their last night in Wales at the Cistercian abbey of Basingwerk, hardly more than a mile north of Holywell town. The ruins of this 'little cell', parts of whose cloister walls date from Gerald's time, are still to be seen.

On Maundy Thursday morning, the cavalcade set out from Basingwerk to ride along the marshy bank of the Dee estuary, traversing ('not without apprehension') an extensive coastal quicksand. To the landward side lay the great wood of Coleshill, where (according to Gerald) Henry II had suffered a most humiliating defeat thirty years earlier. Ignoring the sensible advice of the experienced Marchers who knew the country, the headstrong young monarch had gone plunging off into the wood, slap into a Welsh ambush which cut up his forces disastrously. In his anxiety to score off the king, however, Gerald tells us only part of the story — or perhaps the story as passed on by Prince Dafydd, who had sprung the ambush. As less prejudiced chronicles relate, Henry was indeed attacked in Coleshill wood, but his motive for entering it was not mere wilfulness: the move was in fact designed to outflank a strong Welsh position astride the coast road, and despite the ambush, that is what it eventually achieved. At the end of the day (as Gerald probably knew very well) it was Prince Owain Gwynedd

The Cistercian abbey of Basingwerk, where the mission spent their last night in Wales.

The chapter house at Basingwerk Abbey, extended eastwards in the thirteenth-century.

who had to retreat, not King Henry. Here as elsewhere, then, Gerald proves himself better as a propagandist than a historian. Nor could he resist adding the tear-jerking tale of a young Welshman slain in the battle, whose faithful greyhound guarded his body for eight days, until even the hard-bitten English were shamed into giving it proper burial.

Somewhere south-west of Flint (where Edward I would build a castle to guard the coast road) the travellers themselves doubtless skirted Coleshill wood, passing near the site of Ewloe Castle: a Welsh-built fortress may already have existed there in 1188, but the surviving stone defences were added later by Llywelyn the Great and his grandson, Llywelyn the Last.

By now they were nearing the boundary of Wales, marked here by the winding and as yet uncanalized river Dee. Its sandy fords, Gerald learnt, shifted their position every month as the river altered its course either towards England or Wales, presaging that nation's success or failure in frontier warfare. Splashing across one of these fords, the travellers left behind the land they had traversed so laboriously, and towards the evening of Maundy Thursday, 14 April 1188, they rode into English Chester. Their journey through Wales was over, though their mission to the Welsh people was not quite complete.

The Welsh-built castle of Ewloe, on the edge of Coleshill wood (Photograph by Peter Humphries).

The abbey church of St Werburgh, now Chester Cathedral, where Archbishop Baldwin is likely to have presided over the solemn ceremonies of Easter.

For the time being, nevertheless, they gave themselves over to the solemn ceremonies of Eastertide. Gerald does not tell us exactly where these were performed, but Baldwin most likely presided over services in the Benedictine abbey church of St Werburgh, now Chester Cathedral. Parts of the present building (notably its Norman north transept) still survive from the period of their visit, while very much more remains of the noble Norman interior of St John's church: here, too, the archbishop may have preached one of the sermons which drew many Chester men to take the cross.

In the intervals of ceremonial and recruiting, Gerald clearly found time to enjoy his Easter break. He saw (and probably sampled) the remarkable cheeses which the dowager countess of Chester manufactured from the milk of her pet deer; he collected accounts of local freaks and oddities; and he heard of two mysterious Chester hermits, whose true identity had only been revealed on their death-beds. One was none other than King Harold Godwinson, who had supposedly escaped (albeit lacking an

eye) from his defeat at Hastings: the second ('or so they say') turned out to be the German Emperor Heinrich V, who had allegedly lived for many years in Chester after faking his own death. As Gerald's contemporary readers will have recognized, this last tale had delightfully scandalous overtones, for the emperor was the first husband of Henry II's mother. If he really did survive, her second marriage to the king's father must have been bigamous, so that Henry himself was illegitimate.

The respite in Chester was a short one, for the mission still had unfinished business in hand. So far they had not visited the principality of Powys, which occupied much of northern central Wales — though its boundaries bore little relation to the modern county of the same name. Admittedly, the crusade had already been successfully preached there by Bishop Reiner of St Asaph, but there were also diplomatic complications: the influential Prince Owain Cyfeiliog of southern Powys was less than keen to receive Baldwin, while Gruffudd ap Madog of the north was in bad odour with the Church. It must have seemed desirable, at any rate, to avoid actually entering Powys. For when the travellers rode south from Chester soon after Easter, they literally went out of their way to skirt round its borders, veering south-eastwards through Whitchurch in Shropshire and then south-westwards to Oswestry.

Yet Baldwin was apparently unwilling to abandon Powys altogether. By preaching at Oswestry, just outside its boundaries, he gave the men of the principality a second chance to join the crusade, and perhaps he hoped that Owain Cyfeiliog might change his mind. Owain did not do so, but Gruffudd ap Madog and Eliseg of Penllyn rode in to greet him with many of their followers, and quite a few new Welsh

The stallions of Powys were famous throughout Wales. Three medieval warhorses, from a thirteenth-century bestiary (By permission of the British Library, Harleian Ms. 4751, f.27).

recruits were enlisted. Gruffudd, moreover, publicly repudiated his wife: since she was his first cousin, their marriage was regarded as incestuous by the Church.

Despite this act of conciliation, the mission never set foot in Powys, but Gerald the horse-lover could not refrain from praising its famous breed of stallions. These were descended from Spanish stock introduced by a Norman baron, and they sired splendid-looking horses which were also strong-limbed and astonishingly fast. Nor could he miss the opportunity for a final jibe at Henry II, who had suffered a shattering reverse when he invaded Powys in 1165. For all his costly preparations and well-equipped forces, Henry was forced into ignominious retreat by sudden and torrential rainstorms, and in Gerald's opinion it served him right for plundering Welsh churches and mutilating Welsh hostages.

After their sermon at Oswestry — their very last to a Welsh audience — the travellers were entertained 'in the sumptuous English manner, with

tremendous splendour and style', by the local Norman lord, William fitz Alan. This 'noble and generous'

The great Iron Age hillfort of Old Oswestry, situated close to the mission's route.

The ninth-century Pillar of Eliseg, near Valle Crucis Abbey, commemorates one of the greatest early princes of Powys.

Shrewsbury to Hereford

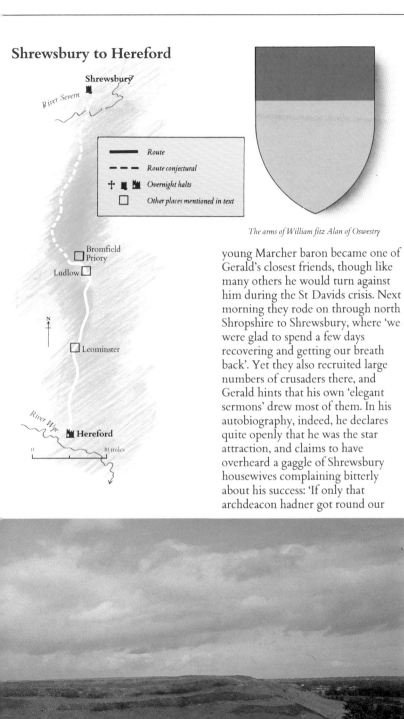

Shrewsbury

River Severn

Bromfield Priory

Ludlow

Leominster

River Wye

Hereford

——	Route
- - -	Route conjectural
✝ ⛪ 🏰	Overnight halts
☐	Other places mentioned in text

N

0   10 miles

The arms of William fitz Alan of Oswestry

young Marcher baron became one of Gerald's closest friends, though like many others he would turn against him during the St Davids crisis. Next morning they rode on through north Shropshire to Shrewsbury, where 'we were glad to spend a few days recovering and getting our breath back'. Yet they also recruited large numbers of crusaders there, and Gerald hints that his own 'elegant sermons' drew most of them. In his autobiography, indeed, he declares quite openly that he was the star attraction, and claims to have overheard a gaggle of Shrewsbury housewives complaining bitterly about his success: 'If only that archdeacon hadner got round our

husbands with his smooth talk, and betwitched them with his innocent looks', one of them lamented, 'they'd have escaped scot-free from all the other preachers'.

They had another, more unpleasant, task to perform. Alone of all the Welsh princes, Owain Cyfeiliog of southern Powys had

A thirteenth-century priest's effigy from Shrewsbury Abbey, showing the bell, book and candle used in excommunication (By courtesy of Shropshire County Library).

shown himself hostile to Baldwin's mission: no doubt he had been warned of the consequences, but he had failed to submit either at Oswestry or Shrewsbury. Now, therefore, the archbishop solemnly excommunicated him with bell, book and candle, cutting him off from all hope of Heaven until he mended his ways. This 'cursing' perhaps took place in Shrewsbury's fine early Norman abbey church of Holy Cross, and Gerald (who gives no reason for Owain's obstinacy) must have attended it with regret, for he clearly admired the prince very much. A wise governor, a fluent talker and a renowned Welsh poet, Owain was an independent-minded man who frequently sided with the Anglo-Normans, and even dared to tease Henry II at the king's own table. Indeed, Gerald numbered him among the foremost native rulers of the age, ranking him alongside the famous Owain Gwynedd and the redoubtable Rhys ap Gruffudd.

The mission was now effectivley over, but there were a few more miles left to travel, and not all easy ones. Riding southward from Shrewsbury towards Wenlock Edge, they had to negotiate the narrow, rugged road called 'Evil Street' — possibly the route through the Church Stretton gap, or perhaps the Portway track over the Long Mynd — before pushing on via Bromfield Priory and 'the noble castle of Ludlow' on its rock high above the Teme. Much of the fortress they saw there still

Right: 'Evil Street' may have passed over the Long Mynd near Church Stretton.

survives, including its unusual round-naved Norman chapel: and so does a substantial portion of Leominster's splendid priory church, which they passed soon after entering Herefordshire.

Twenty years later, Gerald recorded in his autobiography his memories of this last day's journey. He himself rode in the place of honour beside Baldwin, while the archbishop's clerks excitedly discussed the crusade to come,

Below: The Marcher castle and border town of Ludlow.

The round Norman nave of Ludlow Castle chapel, built about 1140.

wondering who would be its best chronicler. To Gerald's immense satisfaction, the archbishop turned towards him: the distinguished author of the *Topography of Ireland*, declared the prelate, was clearly the ideal man to describe the inevitable fall of Saladin and the victory of Christendom. Many of those who had shared their labours during the past weeks — Archdeacon Alexander the interpreter, Bishop Peter and Bishop Saltmarsh, Prince Rhys and the Cistercian abbots — had long since gone their separate ways: but doubtless young William de Barry was riding somewhere near his uncle, and Maelgwn ap Rhys was with them still, still undecided about his crusading vow. With Gerald and Baldwin in the lead and those unsung heroes the servants and packhorsemen bringing up the rear, that evening the travel-stained cavalcade clattered into Hereford. 'And thus, having come full circle, we returned again to the place where we began this difficult journey through Wales'.

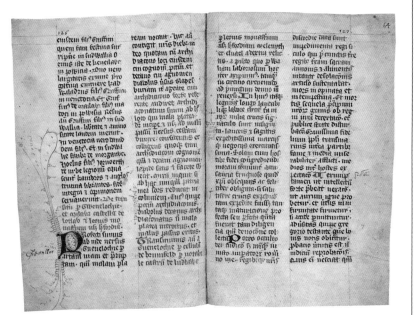

These pages from an early fourteenth-century manuscript of Gerald's Journey through Wales *describe the last days of the mission (By courtesy of the National Library of Wales, Ms. 3024C, ff.63-4).*

Success and Failure
The Journey through Wales and the Third Crusade

Gerald was to declare:

> 'During this long, laborious and praiseworthy mission, about three thousand men were signed with the cross. All of them were very handy with spears and arrows, well experienced in the art of war, and ready to attack the enemies of the faith at the first opportunity . . . If only the crusade itself had proceeded as quickly, and achieved as much success'.

But it did neither, and much of the blame lay with those who had set it in motion, the kings of England and France. Their crusading truce broke down almost as soon as it was concluded, and within two months of Gerald's return to Hereford they were again to open war. Worse still, Prince Richard soon joined King Philip against his own father King Henry, and together they hounded the old English king to an ignominious and despairing death at Chinon on 6 July

The castle of Chinon where Henry II died (Photograph by Peter Humphries).

1189. In the Holy Land, meanwhile, Saladin was busy consolidating his conquests.

At about this time, Gerald had a most disturbing nightmare about Saracens mutilating Christ's body: he was probably feeling guilty about his failure to join the crusade. But the death of his patron King Henry changed everything, for there was now nobody to pay for his journey to

Crusading knights, from a thirteenth-century manuscript produced at Acre (By courtesy of Bibliotheque Nationale, Paris).

Jerusalem, while the new King Richard needed his diplomatic services in Wales. Towards the end of 1189, therefore, he obtained a release from his crusading vow, along with Bishop Peter of St Davids and an unspecified number of Welshmen who had taken the cross. Instead of setting out for the Holy Land, they were ordered to contribute towards crusader funds and also to 'bestow their labour and aid' upon the building of St Davids Cathedral. The great church that stands there today is thus in some measure an enduring memorial to Gerald's preaching tour.

All the same, some of Gerald's Welsh recruits probably accompanied King Richard when he eventually sailed from France in July 1190, three whole years after Saladin's capture of the Holy Cross. So too did Archbishop Baldwin and Ranulf de Glanville, and while Richard delayed yet another year in Sicily and Cyprus, these two valiant old men led a force straight to Palestine, where it brought new heart to the demoralized crusader army besieging Acre. Despite his increasing age and infirmity, indeed, the archbishop became the hero of the hour, commanding the Christian camp and blessing the storming parties as they advanced beneath his holy banner of St Thomas of Canterbury. But within a month of their arrival, de Glanville had succumbed to disease and starvation, and soon afterwards, on 19 November 1190, Baldwin followed him to the grave. Though his end had been hastened by his distress at the debauchery and squalid wrangles of the Christian army, he bequeathed all his possessions to further the crusade he had preached so fervently in Wales.

Baldwin died a hero at the Third Crusade. The entombment of an archbishop, from a thirteenth-century manuscript by Matthew Paris (By permission of the British Library, Royal Ms. C VII, f.117v).

Above: *The church of St Samuel on Mount Joy overlooking Jerusalem. From here, King Richard is said to have caught a distant glimpse of the Holy City (Photograph by R.D. Pringle).*

Left: *King Richard jousting with Saladin — who, like all pagan villains, is depicted with a blue face. From the fourteenth-century Luttrell Psalter (By permission of the British Library, Additional Ms. 42130).*

possession of a string of coastal fortresses, the Lionheart therefore sailed away in September 1192. Having hoped for much but achieved very little, the Third Crusade was over.

Not until King Richard finally arrived in July 1191 did the crusade briefly take fire. Under his brilliant if erratic leadership, the Christians took Acre — afterwards massacring its defenders in cold blood — and twice routed Saladin in battle: but though Richard once rode close enough for a distant view of Jerusalem, he never came near recapturing the Holy City. After concluding a treaty which guaranteed Christian pilgrims access to its shrines, and Christian

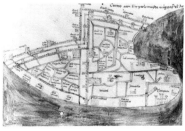

A manuscript map of the city of Acre in 1291 (By courtesy of the Bodleian Library, Ms. Tanner, 190, f.207).

Through no fault of his own, then, Gerald's contribution to the liberation of the Holy Land was minimal. His highly successful preaching tour raised many recruits, but few of them actually reached Palestine, and those that did fell far short of their aim. Yet his involvement in the great crusading movement produced an enduring personal triumph: his *Journey through Wales*, one of the most fascinating and delightful books of the Middle Ages.

Gerald and the Land of Wales

The Natural and Supernatural History of Wales

Gerald was a man of many parts: priest, scholar and reformer; author and traveller; courtier, diplomat and critic of monarchs; by turns Marcher propagandist, agent of English kings and Welsh patriot. Over and above all these things, he was also a man possessed by an insatiable curiosity about the world around him – or, as he called himself, 'a careful investigator of natural history' *(naturalis historiae diligens perscrutator)*. His interpretation of 'natural history' was a wide one: it included not only the ways of birds and beasts and the properties of hills, lakes and standing stones, but also miracles, omens and wonders, the machinations of demons and the revenge of saints. He described the habits of poltergeists in the same matter-of-fact way that he wrote about the habits of beavers, while expressing the same wonder at both, for in Gerald's world both were equally marvellous. For him, indeed, the natural, the apparently unnatural and the supernatural were all part of the same scheme, all demonstrations of the working of God's will.

Mysterious Llangorse Lake, famous for fish, omens and prophecies.

From a modern scientific viewpoint, of course, most of Gerald's writings on natural history are mere fables – but Gerald was not a modern man, and cannot be judged by modern standards. They also had plenty of critics in his own time – but, as usual, Gerald had his answers ready. The Bible, he pointed out, described many things 'which seem incredible or unlikely, but which are nonetheless true': so did the works of great Christian theologians like St Augustine, and the lives of the saints. Were all these to be scorned, simply because they contained miracles and wonders? As the Lord of Nature, moreover, God could do what he liked with His creation. If some of the things he did seemed inexplicable, that

was only because Man was not capable of comprehending His infinite wisdom. Those who cast doubt on the natural marvels Gerald described, in fact, were blasphemously putting a limit on God's power.

Besides, Gerald insisted, he never included anything in his books which he had not either witnessed himself, or 'heard about from reliable men worthy of belief', for 'the surest guide to truth is an eye-witness record'. These 'reliable men' were his downfall – sometimes, indeed, they must have been deliberately leading him on – for the 'natural' history he obtained from such second-hand sources generally strains belief to the utmost. But when Gerald observed

nature with his own eyes, he was often surprisingly accurate, particularly in view of the fact that he was a pioneer in the field, with no reference books to rely on. Those who had previously written about the natural world had done so either for practical reasons (like herbalists or astrologers) or more often as a form of religious instruction – like the authors of pious 'Bestiaries', whose animals symbolized vices and virtues, regardless of their real habits. To study nature for its own sake, as Gerald did, was something new: and for all his credulousness, inconsistency and wild guesswork, he can justly be hailed as the first serious natural historian of Wales.

A Land of Wonders

For Gerald, all Wales was a land of wonders, whose natural features frequently behaved in a most surprising manner. Sometimes these phenomena had an obvious divine purpose - to warn, for instance, of imminent disasters - sometimes they had a logical explanation, and sometimes they defied human explanation altogether. Wells, springs, lakes and rivers (sacred to the pagan Celts and perhaps only cosmetically Christianized by the twelfth century) were particularly given to producing signs and omens, one of the most numinous being Llangorse Lake - which Gerald knew very well, since it lay not far from his home at Llanddew. Though it yielded excellent fish (he noted pike and perch, tench, eels and superb trout) it was much more renowned for its prophetic powers, turning green to presage invasions and sometimes appearing to be ominously streaked with blood.

Even the waterfowl which thronged the lake in winter were clairvoyant: they would only sing at the command of the rightful ruler of the land. This had been dramatically confirmed when Gerald's Welsh great-uncle Prince Gruffudd passed by in the company of two Marcher barons, recently installed as overlords of the region. Neither of these Norman interlopers, however, could raise so much as a twitter from the birds, but when Gruffudd spoke they all began to call at once, beating the water with their wings in their enthusiasm. At this the thunderstruck Marchers galloped away to warn Henry I, who was not in the least surprised. 'By the death of Christ', he swore, 'this is nothing to wonder at. For though our power allows us to inflict great injuries on the Welsh, we know very well that the land is theirs by right'.

According to the locals, moreover, the surface of Llangorse Lake sometimes seemed to be covered with buildings, orchards and gardens (curiously enough, an ancient 'crannog' or artificial island-dwelling came to light when its water level was lowered in the nineteenth century) and when it froze over in winter it 'emitted a horrible noise, as if herds of beasts were bellowing'. This, thought Gerald the objective observer, was probably not sinister at all, but merely due to trapped air escaping through tiny cracks in the ice.

There was also a perfectly natural explanation for a phenomenon which occured at Newgale Sands, near St Davids, and which occasionally occurs there today. The terrible storms of 1172 stripped the beach to reveal the ancient land surface beneath, complete with the stumps of an extensive submerged forest: they were as black as ebony, and the marks of axes still appeared fresh on them. Gerald guessed that they were felled at the time of Noah's Flood, or perhaps somewhat more recently, for he knew from his own experience that the sea continually flooded and eroded the shoreline in this area.

Newgale sands.

He was less confident about the magic properties of the burial mound on Crug Mawr, which the mission passed soon after leaving Cardigan. 'The inhabitants testify', that it miraculously altered its size to match the height of anyone who lay down beside it, while ('it is commonly claimed') any weapons placed upon it at dusk would be found broken to pieces next morning. This mound was clearly an ancient sacred site, and according to the ninth-century writer, Nennius, it also had another power, one particularly relevant to Gerald the traveller: a melancholy pilgrim who knelt before the tumulus three times 'would never be sad again until the day of his death, even if he should journey alone to the ends of the earth'.

Far more marvellous, thought Gerald, was the extraordinary 'homing stone' of Anglesey (which

A pair of prehistoric standing stones at Penrhos Feilw, Holyhead Island, off Anglesey.

once stood in the churchyard of Llanidan, about two miles south of the famous prehistoric tomb of Bryn Celli Ddu. This was shaped like a human thigh, and however far it was taken from its site, it always returned there by the following night. The hard-bitten and cynical Earl Hugh of Shrewsbury, Gerald was assured, had actually tested its powers by chaining it to a much larger stone and dropping it into the sea: but early next morning, it appeared back in its usual place, and the flabbergasted earl ordered that none should ever dare to move it again. Presumably because of its shape, this remarkable stone was also associated with fertility, or rather the reverse. If any couple made love near it ('as has been proved on many occasions') or even 'behaved wantonly', it immediately sweated great drops of water, while no child was ever born as a result of such unions. Neither as a naturalist nor as a Christian could Gerald begin to explain these happenings, and he obviously regarded the thigh-stone as a dangerous, uncanny object, best avoided. A nearby cottage, he observed, had been altogether abandoned, and the monolith itself had been surrounded by a protective wall.

The Creatures of Wales

With notable exceptions, Gerald was at his best when describing birds, beasts and other living creatures, especially those that he observed for himself. If he believed that barnacle geese hatched from barnacle shells, or that summer-visiting birds hibernated in winter, it must be remembered that such theories were commonly held for many centuries after his death: indeed, no scientist visited the barnacle goose's remote Arctic breeding grounds until 1907. Some of the creatures he wrote about,

of course, played an important part in medieval everyday life. Falcons and dogs (which he admired for their loyalty) were used for hunting, while fish were the familiar diet of Fridays and fasting seasons, so that their characteristics, varieties (and taste) were of special interest to a cleric.

Much more remarkable, by twelfth-century standards, was Gerald's concern with wildlife for its own sake. Even on the most gruelling day of his journey through Wales, he took the trouble to note the song of an oriole; he observed that the jackdaws of St Davids were so used to kind treatment from priests that they showed no fear of anyone dressed in

black; and he clearly spent many hours observing the habits of beavers – probably (with a true naturalist's instinct) because he knew them to be already very rare in Britain, surviving only on the Teifi and perhaps on one Scottish river.

What impressed him most was their ingenious method of transporting wood for their dams. One team of beavers gnawed down trees; others turned over on their backs and clutched logs to their bellies with their feet, holding a branch transversely in their teeth; while a third group gripped this branch in their own mouths and hauled the living waggons to the river. Scarcely less wonderful were the dams themselves:

> '. . . which they construct in some deep and tranquil angle of the river, binding the wood together with such skill that no water can drip in: even violent storms scarcely damage them, and they need fear no attack save by humans armed with iron weapons . . . Their wooden fortresses are built so as to project above the usual high-water level: within are passages leading from one storey to the next, and on top they build a platform so that they can keep watch on the rising of the waters when the river is in flood'.

> 'In the river bank by their dams, moreover, they have underground burrows, dry and well-defended hiding places. When a hunter comes looking for them, and strives to thrust his sharpened pole into their dam, the beaver hears the blows and, fearing attack, quickly flees to its stronghold. But first it stirs up the water round the entrance to its hole, scraping away earth with its feet and making the clear transparent stream all cloudy and muddy. Thus it outwits the wily hunter with his iron trident, who is standing on the bank waiting for it to leap out'.

All this is remarkably accurate, and a great credit to Gerald as an observer. Unfortunately, however, he was not content to stick to the evidence of his own eyes, and he could not resist adding another amazing 'fact' about the beaver –

Unrealistic but understandably miserable-looking beavers, shown sacrificing their testicles to hunters. From a thirteenth-century bestiary (By permission of the British Library, Harleian Ms. 4751, f.9v).

though he covered himself by declaring that it only happened 'in Eastern lands'. There (or so he had heard) beavers were much prized for the medicinal properties of their testicles. 'By a marvellous innate understanding'. Eastern beavers were well aware of this, and when hard-pressed by hounds, they would castrate themselves and throw the relevant organs at the hunters, thus literally saving their skins. If a beaver which had made this sacrifice was chased again, it simply ran to a high place and cocked up its hind leg, revealing that the sought-after parts were already missing.

This improbable tale was derived from a pious 'Book of Beasts', where beavers symbolized men who cast away lust to serve God more perfectly. The moral voles of Priestholm (which only ravaged hermits' food when they quarrelled among themselves) probably originated from a similar source, but it is difficult to know what to make of a story Gerald heard in Cemais, where an ill-starred young man called Seisyll Longshanks

'suffered so much persecution from toads on his sickbed, that it seemed as though all the toads of the entire region had made arrangements to assemble there. And though a vast number of them were killed by his friends and those caring for him, yet more and more kept flocking in . . . until nobody could count them. Eventually everyone was worn out . . . so they stripped a tall tree of leaves and branches and hoisted him up into it in a kind of bag. But he was not safe even there from his venomous persecutors. Quite the reverse, for the toads climbed up the tree to look for him, and they killed him and ate him up to the bare bones'.

Gerald himself, indeed, was at a loss to explain this affair. He could only remark darkly that the judgement of God was never unjust, though it was sometimes hard to understand.

Gerald also parted company with probability when he wrote about genetics. He was morbidly fascinated by freaks and hybrids, believing that women could mate with lions and goats, and men with cows – the Breconshire knight who gave birth to a calf, he implied, was being punished for some unnatural vice. He did not, of course, witness this extraordinary delivery, and nor did he actually see the deer-cow, deer-horse and dog-monkey hybrids he describes. Yet he did once meet a Devonshire knight who had inherited his father's battle scars, and knew of another who proved his disputed paternity by inheriting an accidental eye injury. In the light of modern knowledge, of course, all these things are impossible. But to Gerald they were simply examples of 'nature at play', wonders through which she demonstrated that (like the power of God) she was capable of feats far beyond human comprehension.

Some of Gerald's genetic freaks and hybrids, including a deer-cow and a woman mating with a lion. From a thirteenth-century manuscript of his Topography of Ireland *(By permission of the British Library, Royal Ms. 13 B VIII).*

Demons, Prophets and Fairies

For most twentieth-century people, the supernatural beings which populated Gerald's world seem even more improbable than his 'natural' freaks and hybrids. But to Gerald they were as real as beavers, if not always as visible: like most medieval men, he believed that devils enjoyed a certain license from God to tempt humankind, and while their power had been much diminished by the coming of Christ, it was still a force to be reckoned with. Though given to visions, Gerald does not appear to have had any first-hand contacts with 'unclean spirits'. His Pembroke neighbours, however, were much plagued by what would now be called poltergeists. One of these cut up people's clothes, even if they were carefully locked away, but another (which inhabited the house of Stephen Wiriet, probably Orielton near Pembroke) had an embarrassing habit of arguing with humans, and if provoked would publicly reveal nasty little secrets about them. Such spirits, thought Gerald, were mischievous rather then really harmful, yet they were also extraordinarily resistant to exorcism: priests armed with crucifixes and holy water, indeed, were particularly likely to be pelted with filth.

These poltergeists were invisible, but demons sometimes took human form, and the kind known as 'incubi' specialized in affairs with mortal women - Gerald knew of one in the Chepstow area which used to chat to its mistress's neighbours. Such unions, moreover, could produce half-human offspring, like Merlin of Carmarthen or a certain Simon, who obtained a post as steward at Stackpole Elidor, a few miles west of Gerald's Manorbier. Apart from his ominous red hair and the fact that he never went to church, there seemed nothing strange about him at first. Indeed, he proved almost the perfect steward: the estate prospered, and his employers had

Exorcism was rarely effective against poltergeists. Two exorcizing priests sprinkling holy water, from the Sherbrooke Missal, about 1320 (By courtesy of the National Library of Wales, Ms. 15536 E, f.334).

only to think of something they wanted for it to appear, though he often reproached them for scrimping and saving: what was the point, when they could not take it with them?

Before long he was controlling the place altogether, serving the labourers and hired hands with the best of everything and generally doing exactly as he liked. Then, by chance,

The church of Stackpole Elidor, which the demon steward never entered (By courtesy of the National Monuments Record, Wales).

someone saw him 'conversing by night near the mill pond' - presumably with invisible fellow-spirits - and the next morning he was dismissed: however efficient they might be, demons could clearly not be employed about the house. He then revealed that he was the son of a local woman by an incubus which appeared in the guise of her husband, and his mother confirmed the story.

Mortal men likewise fell victim to devils in the form of beautiful women. One fine Palm Sunday evening, Meilyr of Caerleon met a girl he had long desired in a pleasant country spot: but as soon as he began making love to her, she immediately turned into a hairy monster of horrible aspect. Not surprisingly, the shock sent Meilyr raving mad, and though he was eventually nursed back to health at St Davids, he never lost he ability to see and converse with demons and to foretell the future with their aid. Apparently their powers of prophecy were

An assortment of devils emerge from hell-mouth to attack St Guthlac. From the twelfth-century Guthlac Roll (By permission of the British Library, Harley Roll Y 6).

limited, for they were often wrong about events distant either in time or place. Their principal duty, indeed, was to entrap human souls, and Meilyr often saw them as horn-carrying huntsmen – especially around churches and monasteries, the front line of the conflict between good and evil. They also appeared dancing on the tongues of liars, or hovering around books which contained misleading statements: great swarms of them – claimed Gerald, who never could resist a crack at his fellow 'historian' – invariably covered Geoffrey of Monmouth's *History of the Kings of Britain*, but they could be put to flight by the production of St John's Gospel.

Meilyr's demons betrayed him in the end, assuring him that he would escape with only a wound from the Norman attack on Usk Castle in 1174: so he did, but the wound killed him soon afterwards. It is therefore unlikely that Gerald ever met him, but he clearly made a study of other Welsh soothsayers -*awenyddion* or

'inspired poets', as he calls them in his *Description of Wales*. When consulted about some problem, they would immediately pass into a trance and pour out a torrent of confused words: only by carefully interpreting these would the enquirer obtain his reply, and if he asked a second or third time he would get different answers altogether. When shaken out of their trance, moreover, these soothsayers remembered nothing they had said, recalling only that some sweet substance seemed to have been smeared on their lips, or a sheet of writing pressed against their mouths. Though they always invoked the Holy Trinity before they prophesied, Gerald half suspected that they were possessed by some kind of evil spirit: on the other hand, he knew plenty of examples of true prophecies inspired by God, including those of his beloved Merlin Silvester.

He had also heard of other mysterious beings, neither poltergeists, demons, nor prophetic

spirits: they should perhaps be classified as fairies, though Gerald simply calls them 'men of tiny stature'. They inhabited the Swansea area – renowned for its fairies until Methodists drove them out in the nineteenth century – where a boy named Elidyr met two of them while hiding by a riverbank. Having followed them down an underground passage to a beautiful twilight land, he was presented to their king and became the playmate of their prince. Though 'no bigger than pygmies', they were perfectly formed, with long fair hair flowing over their shoulders, and they rode horses about the size of greyhounds. They never ate meat or fish, but only milk dishes flavoured with saffron; they never swore oaths; and they never lied – indeed, the worship of truth was the only religion they practised.

Elidyr was allowed to pass from their world to ours as he pleased, until one day his mother asked him to bring her some of their abundant gold. So he carried off the prince's golden ball, but as he reached her threshold he tripped and dropped it into the hands of the hotly pursuing pygmies, who ran away with jeers of derision. After that he could never find the entrance to the twilight land again, and he remained ashamed of his action even as an ageing priest, crying whenever he recounted his story to Gerald's uncle Bishop David. He also told the bishop (who passed it on to his nephew) that the little men spoke a tongue rather like Greek: Gerald thought it might have been an ancient form of Welsh, which he (wrongly) believed to be directly derived from that language.

Whether the story was actually true was another matter. 'if you ask me', wrote Gerald,

'. . . I can only reply with St Augustine that divine miracles are to be wondered at, not argued about or analysed. I will neither put a limit on divine power by denying it, nor strain the bounds of credibility by accepting it . . . Stories like this can neither be fully confirmed nor rejected out of hand'.

Saints and Miracles

If Gerald was unsure about the existence of fairies, he had no doubts at all about saints and miracles. Saints were holy men and women, and the miracles they performed either during their lives or after death demonstrated both their own sanctity and 'the wonderful power of God'. There was no question whatever that miracles occurred, and occurred quite frequently. No less than four times during the journey through Wales, indeed, God displayed His power directly: by curing the old woman of Haverfordwest; by inspiring Gerald's uncomprehending audience there; and by punishing the Cardigan woman and the scornful young aristocrats of Anglesey. More often, however, He operated through His saints. Gerald's books are full of their miracles, and wrote at least five saints' lives, including those of St David (of course) and of Caradoc of Rhos (d.1124), a holy Pembrokeshire hermit also enshrined in St Davids Cathedral.

This last was compiled as part of a campaign to get Caradoc officially canonized: in 1199 Gerald read it to Pope Innocent in Rome, and persuaded him to set the process in motion. The original manuscript is lost, but surviving extracts suggest that Caradoc's miracles were numerous. He healed dropsical tumours with a touch, turned herrings into pennies for the poor, and immobilized the ship of some Vikings who tried to kidnap him: while his coffin was being carried across Newgale Sands to St Davids, it stayed bone-dry despite a violent rainstorm, and his body remained uncorrupted for many years – a sure sign of divine favour. When the historian William of Malmesbury tried to cut off one of its fingers as a personal relic, indeed, the saintly corpse horrified him by jerking its hand away.

Fortunately for William, Caradoc was an unusually forbearing saint, who took no revenge. In general, however, the saints of Wales were almost as posthumously touchy as those of Ireland, whom Gerald called the most vindictive in the world. They jealously guarded the churches dedicated to them, which were

The head of the fourteenth-century effigy of Caradoc of Rhos, from his tomb-shrine in St Davids Cathedral (Photograph by Roger Vlitos).

accordingly held in great awe: that was the reason, thought Gerald, why Welsh churches were always so much more tranquil than those of other lands.

Twice, he reported, brash Norman hunters who turned such sanctuaries into makeshift hound-kennels were miraculously punished, the castellan of Radnor by blindness and Earl Hugh by an arrow in the eye. A boy from Llanfaes near Brecon was lucky to escape with a fright. With amazing temerity, he tried to steal some young doves from a nest in St David's church there, doves being that saint's sacred birds: but his hand stuck fast to a stone in the wall, and only after three anxious days and nights of fasting and prayer was it eventually released. There was no doubt that this had actually occurred, for Gerald heard the tale from the boy himself many years later, while the stone bearing his finger-marks ('as if pressed into wax') was long displayed at Llanfaes as a relic.

Objects associated with the saints, moreover, were almost as powerful and dangerous as the saints themselves. 'Handbells, staffs crooked at the top and plated with gold and silver or bronze, and all kinds of other relics of the saints', Gerald wrote,

'. . . are regarded with great reverence by the clergy and people not only of Ireland and Scotland, but also of Wales. In fact, they are much more frightened of breaking the oaths they swear on these things than those they swear on the Gospels. This is because such objects are possessed of some hidden power instilled in them by God: besides, the particular saint who finds them especially pleasing will take vengeance on all who scorn them, savagely punishing all oathbreakers'.

Thus, for example, the man who struck St Cynog's gilded torc was immediately struck blind in both eyes, and even Prince Rhys ap Gruffudd was not exempt from its retaliation. Because he carried it off from Merthyr Cynog and shut it up in Dinefwr Castle, he himself was captured and locked away at Nevern. Just as salutary was the vengeance of St Patrick's horn, which Gerald apparently witnessed himself. This bronze horn used to be carried about Breconshire by a wandering Irish beggar, who offered it to be kissed by the faithful: out of reverence for its former saintly owner, however, no one had ever dared to blow it, until a foolish priest named Bernard set it to his lips and sounded a great blast. At once his mouth became paralysed, and though he had previously been an eloquent, hectoring man, he was seized with a lifelong speech impediment – in modern terms, he had a stroke. What was worse, he almost entirely lost his memory: he could hardly recall his own name; he forgot the psalms he had known by heart; and Gerald was amazed to see him struggling to re-learn his alphabet, like some senile schoolboy.

In the end, Bernard partly recovered his health by making a penitent pilgrimage to St Patrick's Irish shrine. Such pilgrimages – the longer and more arduous the better – were a well-established method of mollifying or currying favour with the saints. According to Gerald, the myriad holy places of Rome were the favourite goal of Welsh pilgrims, and in 1206 he himself travelled there a fourth time,

> 'solely by way of pilgrimage, so that by the labours of the journey, by almsgiving and by true confession . . . he might wipe away the stains of his past life'.

There were, however, plenty of famous shrines in Wales itself, like tombs of St David and Caradoc the hermit at St Davids and of St Beuno at Clynnog Fawr in Gwynedd, or the holy well of St Winefred (still a thriving pilgrimage - centre today) in Clwyd: as well as hundreds of lesser, more remote shrines like that of the hare-protecting St Melangell, at Pennant Melangell in the Powys Berwyns, or of St Issui at Partrishow in the Black Mountains. All these survive in some form, and they are perhaps the best keys we have to Gerald's twelfth-century world of wonder and belief.

Right: *The reconstructed twelfth-century shrine of St Melangell, in Pennant Melangell church, Powys.*

Below: *St Winefred's healing well, encased in its splendid late fifteenth-century shrine-chapel, at Holywell, Clwyd.*

The priest Bernard foolishly blows St Patrick's Horn, from a thirteenth-century manuscript of Gerald's Topography of Ireland *(By permission of the British Library, Royal Ms. 13 B VII).*

The Archaeology of Gerald's Wales
by David M. Robinson

The Norman barons and their followers continued to etch a deep imprint upon Wales in the later twelfth century. In both the March and in the native north and west, the period was one of major transformation. Profound changes were taking place in the material basis of Welsh society, the nature of the economy and the pattern of settlement — areas all of great interest to the archaeologist. Gerald was by far the most widely travelled and acute observer of Wales at this time and, used with care, his informed comments provide illuminating insights into some of the archaeological implications of this change.

It would be wrong, however, to accept Gerald's oft-quoted passage from the *Description of Wales* as a universal truth:

> 'They do not live in towns, villages, or castles, but cling to the woods like hermits. It is their custom to raise on the edge of woods not great, high palaces or sumptuous and superfluous buildings of stone and mortar, but wattle huts, sufficient for one year's use, involving only moderate effort and cost'.

In fact, this can be taken as no more than a broad indication, and must be weighed against the current evidence from archaeology. The present situation allows for no more than a basic framework, but one upon which archaeologists continue to build.

The commote of Iâl was annexed by Owain Gwynedd in the late 1140s, and henceforth it was protected by one of the finest Welsh earthwork castles, Tomen y Rhodwydd. This aerial view shows the motte and bailey from the south-east (Photograph by Peter Humphries).

Although Gerald says that the Welsh did not live in towns, he was clearly aware of the existence of urban centres in the March. Cardiff, Kidwelly and Pembroke, for example, were all flourishing boroughs in his day. Moreover, in the heart of Wales, the Anglo-Norman influence had led to change. The Lord Rhys held the former Norman borough at Llandovery, and at Cardigan in 1188 (p. 53), he must have played host to the mission at a centre with many of the attributes of urban life. Few would accept that *all* of the occupants and traders in these towns were immigrants.

A reconstruction of the 'ringwork' castle at Castle Tower, Penmaen, based on excavations at the site. Although earth and timber castles remained the norm in the twelfth-century March, stone became increasingly common at most major Marcher and royal strongholds (Illustration by Terry Ball).

The castle, too, was by no means alien to the Welsh princes of the later twelfth century. They had begun to imitate the Norman example soon after 1100, and earthwork motte and bailey strongholds gradually spread throughout the princely territories. By the middle of the century, Owain Gwynedd had built Tomen y Rhodwydd, as fine a castle as many of its contemporaries in the March. More telling, perhaps, is Gerald's emphasis upon the two new stone castles at Castell Aber Ia and Carn Fadryn (p. 63). True, from excavations at Tomen Castell (Dolwydellan) and Dinas Emrys (which have revealed the bases of rectangular towers), it seems the princes could build in masonry at this time. Nevertheless, Gerald's observations in Gwynedd suggests that stone was still relatively novel in Welsh castles by 1188.

Even in Norman areas, earth and timber still predominated, as at Kidwelly or at the much smaller ringwork excavated at Penmaen, Gower. Yet, here again, great changes were taking place. At Rumney, a site mentioned by Gerald in the *Description*, detailed

A view of the excavations at Rumney Castle, Glamorgan. The mission of 1188 must have passed very close to this site on route between Newport and Cardiff. At the time, a stone keep had probably just been added to an essentially timber stronghold (By courtesy of the Glamorgan-Gwent Archaeological Trust).

excavations have uncovered evidence of a stone keep added to an essentially timber stronghold. Indeed, a 'transition to stone' was occurring at most major Marcher and royal castles in this period, including those at Cardiff, Usk (pp. 35, 39) and White Castle. Gerald would have been well placed to observe the same change at Brecon, for example, or possibly at his family home of Manorbier.

Gerald's description of Welsh housing may also be misleading and should be treated with some caution. It would seem to apply more convincingly to temporary upland summer houses (*hafotai*) such as those excavated on Gelligaer Common, Glamorgan, in the 1930s. The materials used in permanent dwellings no doubt varied according to the area. Excavations at deserted village sites in the Vale of Glamorgan, including Barry and Highlight, suggest that wood was probably used for peasant houses in

the earlier twelfth century. There is, however, evidence that dry-stone masonry was used in 'manorial' buildings, and that by 1200 this had extended to lesser dwellings. Further west, at Rhossili, a particularly large peasant house of this period has been uncovered. It showed signs of internal divisions, and the walls were bonded with clay. In Gwynedd, at Cefn Graeanog, a substantial farmstead was recently excavated (p. 91) and there the evidence suggests a shift from wholly timber construction, to buildings with stone footings, about 1200.

Excavations at Cefn Graeanog, Guynedd, revealed the remains of a substantial twelfth to thirteenth-century farmstead, comprising a house, barn, stable and byre. The house was preceded by an earlier timber building (Photograph by R.S. Kelly, Gwynedd Archaeological Trust).

It is difficult to generalize about the artefacts in everyday use within Welsh homes, though Gerald's comments are again invaluable (pp. 90–2). Pottery was certainly becoming more abundant, and though higher quality vessels were still imported, there were several production centres within Wales. The Monnow valley, the Vale of Glamorgan, and the central Marches were all producing various forms of pottery by 1200. In parts of native Wales, wooden bowls and other vessels probably continued to play an important part at this time.

Finally, cathedrals, monastic houses and churches were also undergoing great change during Gerald's lifetime. Three of the cathedral churches visited by the mission in 1188 saw substantial rebuilding programmes in the later twelfth century. At St Davids this work was actually in progress during Gerald and Baldwin's visit. Again, at Strata Florida, where the Lord Rhys had recently assumed the patronage, they are likely to have encountered builders' scaffolding around the shell of a new abbey church.

A great deal of archaeological work remains to be done on this period. Nevertheless, a combination of the results, together with the insights provided by Gerald of Wales, offers a rare and potentially rewarding challenge for the future.

Gerald and the People of Wales

Three-quarters Norman and a quarter Welsh, Gerald belonged to the land of Wales, but not to the Welsh people: though he was *Giraldus Cambrensis*, 'Gerald of Wales', he was never entirely *Gerallt Cymro*, 'Gerald the Welshman'. He was, rather, 'Gerald the Marcher', a member of a race which (despite their French speech and largely Norman descent) regarded Wales as their homeland, yet remained quite separate from its native inhabitants.

His attitude to those inhabitants, therefore, was always ambiguous, though it developed with the viscissitudes of his career. As a still-hopeful servant of the English kings, he could suggest that the entire native population of Wales should be deported to make room for more tractable colonists. 'Some people', he continued,

> '. . . judge that it would be even safer and wiser to abandon such a rough and trackless country (whose inhabitants are quite untameable) to wild animals, and turn it into a game preserve'.

In later editions of his work, however, he suppressed this astounding piece of racial arrogance, and as he became more and more embittered by the prejudice against his own Welsh connections, so he grew progressively more sympathetic to the Welsh people. At the height of his struggle for St Davids, indeed, he was at least temporarily a fully-fledged Welsh patriot, who boasted that:

> 'Our British race . . . defending their liberty against both Saxons and Normans by continual rebellion, has up until today thrown off the yoke of servitude by strength and arms'.

Gerald's equivocal position is reflected by his *Description of Wales*, one of the most accomplished of all his books. This pioneering account of 'our Wales and its people, so very different and distinct from all other

nations', was written as a tribute to the land of his birth. But he was determined to be impartial about its native inhabitants, dwelling on their manifold vices as well as their virtues: and he ends with two chapters on how the Anglo-Normans could best conquer and hold down the Welsh, balanced by a single (much shorter) section on how the Welsh could resist and rebel against the Anglo-Normans.

Like many of his other writings, of course, the *Description* contains its share of fables. For example, Gerald firmly believed that the Welsh (a name he rightly disliked, since it came from the Anglo-Saxon *wealas*, meaning 'foreigners') were the descendants of refugees from the siege of Troy. In his opinion, their correct name of 'Cambrians' (really *cymry*, 'fellow-countrymen') was derived from a mythical Trojan leader called Camber, while their language was a version of the Greek they picked up during their post-siege travels. Some of his statements about Welsh life, moreover, are only partially true. He declares that they consumed much meat and milk, but little bread: yet bread-corn was widely grown in the lowlands, and Gerald himself noted the wheatfields of Anglesey. He says that they built

Anglesey, granary of Wales.

no castles, yet in 1188 he stayed in at least one Welsh-built castle, and described two more in Gwynedd. Such relatively minor faults apart, Gerald's *Description* provides us with an invaluable and fascinating picture of the people of twelfth-century Wales.

The Welsh at Home

What struck Gerald most forcibly about Welsh domestic life was its extreme frugality. On most days, he relates, the Welsh were content with a single, modest meal in the evening, and sometimes not even that — if there happened to be no food available, they just fasted patiently until the next evening. Nor did they spend much on clothes: whatever the weather, they wore only a thin cloak over a shirt, presumably leaving the feet and legs bare, like Cynwrig ap Rhys, (p. 56). These thin cloaks were the hallmark of a Welshman, and

A thirteenth-century north Wales spearman, wearing a thin cloak over a long shirt. His right foot is bare, perhaps to give it added purchase on the ground when he throws his spear, and he also carries a long knife (From the Littere Wallie — *Copyright: Public Record Office, E36/274).*

according to the *Speculum Duorum* they were 'covered with stripes of various multicoloured cloths' — in other words, they were plaid or tartan, and like the Scottish Highland 'great plaid' they were sometimes worn draped over the head, with the bottom right hand corner thrown over the left shoulder.

Though far from dressy, the Welsh took considerable pains with their personal appearance. Both sexes cut their hair in a 'round tonsure' (or 'pudding-basin' style) above their eyes and ears, and the women then covered it with a flowing white veil, 'raised up in folds like a crown'. Some men, however, shaved their heads bare ('for ease in running through thickets') and all shaved their chins, leaving a moustache on the upper lip. In this, Gerald pointed out, they perpetuated the fashion of the moustachioed Britons described by Julius Caesar, and like them they were most particular about shaving the lower parts of their bodies. 'Above all other nations', moreover, they took great care of their teeth, continually rubbing them with green hazel twigs and polishing them with woollen cloths until they shone like ivory.

The homes of the Welsh were as modest as their diet and clothing. Gerald claimed that they inhabited neither towns, villages or castles, preferring a hermit-like existence on the edges of woods: nor did they build sumptuous palaces or luxurious stone mansions, making do with cheap and labour-saving huts of interwoven branches which kept the weather out all the year round

An artist's impression of a Welsh farmstead, about 1200, based on excavations (see pp. 88-9) at Cefn Graeanog (Illustration by Roger Jones).

(pp. 88-9). Into these homes, however, they welcomed all comers, for the Welsh were even more renowned for hospitality than for frugality. 'There are no beggars among this race', declared Gerald, and Walter Map confirmed 'they are exceedingly generous with their goods, very sparing of food to themselves and lavish with it to others, so that everyone's food is everyone else's'.

Once inside, guests would be entertained all day long by young girls playing harps — unlike the insanely jealous Irish, the Welsh did not hide their women away. Men also played the harp, which they regarded as the highest

An Irish harper, from a twelfth-century manuscript of Gerald's Topography of Ireland (By courtesy of the National Library of Ireland, Ms. 700).

of all skills. Their fingering was extraordinarily rapid, and they produced soft and subtle harmonies, playing in fourths or fifths but always beginning and ending in B flat so as to round off the melody. They likewise played the flute and the *crwth* — a kind of bowed

Thirteenth-century bone flute, from White Castle, Gwent (By permission of the National Museum of Wales).

lyre — and, of course, they sang.

'Unlike the folk of other regions', observed Gerald,

'. . . the Welsh do not sing their traditional songs in unison, but in many parts, and in many modes and modulations. So that in a choir of singers — a customary thing among these people — you will hear as many different parts and voices as you see heads: but in the end they all join together in a smooth and sweet B-flat resonance and melodic harmony'.

So attached to harmony were the Welsh, indeed, that they never sang simple tunes: and what was even more remarkable, Welsh infants naturally sang in parts from the moment they stopped squalling.

When evening came, guests would be served with the single meal of the day, while their host and hostess stood by: these never ate until everyone else had finished, and if there was any shortage, it was they who suffered. Twelfth-century Welsh cooking did not run to varied dishes or appetising dainties, and

A tripod pitcher of about 1220, imported to Loughor Castle (By permission of the National Library of Wales).

the meal was likely to consist of some combination of meat, oats, milk, butter and cheese, with unhopped ale or cider. Neither did anyone bother about table manners. Indeed, there were no tables, tablecloths or napkins, and the diners sat (presumably on the floor) in groups of three, not in pairs as elsewhere: this, says Gerald, they did in honour of the Trinity, having learnt the custom from early Christian missionaries. Then all the courses were served at once in large bowls or platters set upon rushes and fresh herbs, though sometimes meat broth might be ladled onto *lagana* (or 'trenchers') of fresh bread, rolled out thin and baked on a griddle.

However plain the meal, the accompanying conversation was almost certain to be lively. For the Welsh, Gerald proclaimed, were the shrewdest and quickest-witted of all Western peoples, loving poetry and valuing wit highly. They delighted in word-play, double-meanings and especially in sly, sarcastic comments, sometimes light-hearted but often extremely biting — Welsh humour has apparently not changed much over the centuries! Shy, silent Welshmen, Gerald thought, were very rare: most would speak up confidently, however exalted the company — unlike the oafish, tongue-tied English, who inherited their pale colouring and cold-bloodedness from their icy northern ancestry, whereas the Welsh derived their dark complexion and quick temper from the baking plains of Troy.

Welshmen high and low were also addicted to reciting their pedigrees, which they knew by heart: given half a chance, they would reel off the names of their forbears to the sixth or seventh generation, or even beyond. This obsession with noble ancestry, though honourable in itself, had its darker side. Being naturally vindictive and blood-thirsty, the Welsh would brutally avenge any wrong done even to their distant kin, however long ago it occurred. Nor did it prevent savage feuds between brothers (such as

Gerald deplored in Gwynedd and elsewhere) which were exacerbated by the Welsh custom of dividing a father's lands between all his sons. The fact that 'they would much rather marry into a noble family than a rich one', moreover, led to what Gerald regarded as one of the worst Welsh vices — that of 'incest' or marrying close cousins, so as to preserve the family genes. This, of course, was against Church law, as was the Welsh customary divorce system, which Gerald misinterpreted as

'. . . buying young girls from their parents for a fixed payment, and with an agreed financial penalty for changing their minds'.

The witticisms and pedigree-reciting over, guests and family alike retired to the communal bed: which, like Welsh food, clothes and housing, was scarcely luxurious. 'This is placed along one wall of the house' (wrote Gerald, seemingly from bitter personal experience)

'. . . and is stuffed only with a few thin rushes, while its only covering is a stiff coarse blanket, which they weave locally and call a *brychan*. Everyone goes to bed fully clothed . . . a fire is kept burning all night at their feet, and they also get much warmth from the people sleeping close by them. If the side they lie on begins to ache from the hardnness of the bed, or their uppermost side gets frozen with cold, they just get up and go to the fire, whose heat soon dispels both discomforts. Then they go back to bed, where they keep turning over, subjecting alternate sides to the cold and to the unyielding hardness'.

A thirteenth-century south Wales archer, with 'rough-looking and unformed' short bow. He wears the distinctly Welsh thin cloak and long shirt, and his right foot is bare to give him added grip and stability when shooting (From the Littere Wallie *— Copyright: Public Record Office, E36/274).*

The Welsh at War

'The Welsh', declared Gerald, 'are extreme in all they do: so that if you never meet anyone worse than a bad Welshman, you will never meet anyone better than a good one'. They were, for example, extremely hardy, extremely generous and extremely witty: yet they were also extremely treacherous, extremely revengeful and extremely greedy for land. But above all they were passionately devoted to liberty, and almost excessively warlike.

Fighting, in fact, was the only thing they really cared about. Thus they shunned trade and craftsmanship, and ploughed the land only once a year. Instead, they devoted themselves to caring for their horses and weapons, to military training, and to keeping fit for war by climbing mountains and tracking through woods, while their frugal way of life rendered them naturally tough. What was more, they were a whole nation in arms. Unlike the people of Norman England, sharply divided into a military aristocracy and a mass of unwarlike peasants, every single Welshman was ready for battle at a moment's notice.

This universal preparedness had much to do with the Welsh method of fighting. Unlike Norman heavy cavalrymen, they needed neither costly full armour nor expensive, lengthily trained warhorses. They were, wrote Gerald, fierce rather than strong, relying on agility rather than brute force and manoeuvrability rather than irresistible weight. So they wore only the minimum protection — perhaps a light mail shirt, a helmet and a small round shield, but leg armour only rarely. Indeed, they seldom wore shoes, and because of the mountainous or marshy nature of their land they generally fought on foot. Welsh princes, however, might ride fast well-bred horses into battle, and the whole army could speedily mount up if it came to pursuit or flight.

The classic Welsh weapons were likewise those of the light infantryman — the spear and the bow. Very long spears were popular in the north, and especially in Merioneth: these could be thrust straight through chain mail, and could also be thrown as javelins. In south Wales, however, the bow prevailed, the men of Gwent being the best archers in the country. 'Their bows', Gerald observed,

> '. . . are not made of horn, sapwood or yew, but merely of wych elm — not shaped or polished, but rough-looking and unformed. Yet they are stiff and strong, and though they cannot fire arrows very far, they inflict deadly wounds at close range'.

Thirteenth-century spearhead from Laugharne Castle, Dyfed (Photograph by Richard Avent).

Heavily armoured Norman knights, from the Bayeux Tapestry. Their charge was devastating in open country, but they were far less effective among the mountains of Wales.

These were not, then, the far-shooting longbows later made famous by the Welsh archers of the Hundred Years War, but they were much feared by the Normans. The veteran Marcher warrior William de Braose (p. 32), told Gerald how

> '. . . one of his soldiers, in a battle against the Welsh, was struck by a Welsh arrow in the thigh. It penetrated through his padded cloth hauberk and right through his leg armour, and this same arrow then passed on through his saddle flap and deep into his horse, mortally wounding it. Another soldier was likewise hit by an arrow which penetrated through his hauberk and leg armour and into his saddle. When he reined his horse round in a half circle, moreover, a second arrow shot by the same archer hit him in the other thigh, so that he was firmly fixed to his horse on both sides. What more could you expect, even from a crosbow?'

The fact that they were lightly armoured and on foot, indeed, did not deter the Welsh from attacking (and sometimes beating) heavily armoured Norman cavalry. Their first assault, Gerald reported, could be quite terrifying, for they yelled, glowered and made a horrible noise with their long high-pitched trumpets, showering the enemy with volleys of javelins before charging in at a run. But if steadfastly resisted, they soon turned to flee, pausing to fire arrows over their shoulders — 'the Parthian shot' — as they went. All their battles, then, swiftly turned either into pursuits or flights: they were quite incapable of fighting on flat land or of maintaining a hand to hand struggle for very long, much preferring to wear down the enemy by ambushes and sudden night attacks.

In short, the Welsh were guerillas fighting on their own terms, and as such almost impossible to defeat decisively.

> 'For though they may be routed today, and shamefully put to flight with great slaughter, yet tomorrow they are ready for another campaign, quite undaunted by their losses and humiliation . . . They are deterred neither by hunger or cold, fighting does not exhaust them, nor adversity cause them to despair: after an overthrow they immediately rise again, ready to face the hazards of warfare once more. Thus it is easy to beat them in a single battle, but very difficult indeed to win a war against them'.

Conquest or Resistance?

How, then, could Wales be finally conquered? Sprung from generations of Marcher warriors and himself extremely interested in warfare, Gerald was ready with his advice. Any king of England who wished to subdue Wales, he counselled, must first and foremost rely on Marcher troops. These men knew the country, they were almost as hardy as the Welsh, and they could beat them at their own game: being lightly-armed and highly adaptable, they could serve either as horsemen or infantry, and thus pursue the enemy wherever he fled. Specialized Norman or French heavy cavalry were all very well in their own lands, but in Wales they were quite useless, for:

> 'There they fight on plains, here in rough terrain; they fight in fields, we in woods; there armour is honourable, here it is a nuisance; they win by standing firm, we by agility; they capture the enemy, we cut off his head; they ransom prisoners, we slaughter them'.

So if Wales was ever to be conquered, it would be by the Marchers, the heirs of the men who first invaded it.

Even with Marcher aid, the king of England must be prepared for a long and costly war, for the Welsh could neither be beaten in a single battle nor trapped behind fortifications. He should take advantage of their notorious feuds and sow dissension among them, and at the same time use his fleet to blockade their coast, cutting off the foreign imports upon which they relied. Then, when Welsh supplies were at their scarcest in the late winter, he must send light-armed troops to penetrate their woodland fastnesses: casualties on both sides would be heavy, but there was plenty of money in England to hire fresh mercenaries, whereas Welsh losses could not be replaced. He should likewise build, provision and garrison a series of strong castles, 'not only in the Marches, but also at carefully selected points in the interior': and keep the borderlands in a constant state of war-readiness, creating there a nation in arms of his own. When finally conquered, moreover, the Welsh must be governed fairly but firmly: their revolts must be mercilessly crushed, and though they should be respected in defeat, they must never be trusted.

King Edward I, the conqueror of Wales, with his bishops and senior churchmen. From a manuscript of about 1285 (By permission of the British Library, Cotton Vitellius Ms. A XIII).

Beaumaris, the last-built and most technically perfect of Edward I's Welsh Castles, was intended to control Anglesey.

Nearly a century later, Edward I's conquest of Wales would follow Gerald's programme remarkably closely. Unlike previous kings of England, Edward used the entire overwhelming resources of his nation to fight a long, carefully planned war. He sent Marcher columns to strike deep into Wales, exploited the rivalries between Welsh princes, and used his fleet to raid the rich harvest of Anglesey, thus starving out his enemy Llywelyn the Last of Gwynedd. And, of course, he built his famous castles 'not only in the Marches but also . . . in the interior'. Indeed, he ringed the conquered territory with no less than ten new royal fortresses — notably Flint, Rhuddlan, Conwy, Caernarfon, Harlech and Beaumaris — supported by four Marcher castles (including Denbigh) and three rebuilt Welsh strongholds, Dolwyddelan, Criccieth and Castell-y-Bere.

Caernarfon Castle, the showiest of Edward's Welsh fortresses, was designed to proclaim his imperial power.

Harlech, probably the strongest of Edward I's castles of the conquest.

'Because I am descended from both races', Gerald wrote in the final chapter of his *Description of Wales*,

'. . . reason dictates that I should now argue the opposite point of view . . . and give the Welsh some brief but useful advice on the art of resistance'.

Brief it was, but not all useful: if the Welsh had adopted the alien Norman manner of fighting in heavy armour and ordered ranks, as he suggested, they would have thrown away every natural advantage they possessed. Much more valuable was his counsel that the Welsh princes should stand firmly together in defence of their nation — or better still, that the whole Welsh nation should unite behind one single ruler, 'and he a good one'. If only they would do so, Gerald could not see how so very strong, hardy and warlike a people, fighting for survival in a land so well defended by nature, could ever be completely defeated. In the end, did Gerald hope that they would be, and where did his sympathies really lie? Perhaps it is significant that he put the last words of his book into the mouth of an old Welshman, who was nevertheless fighting against his own people in the service of Henry II. When asked what the final outcome of the war would be, he replied

'My lord king, this nation may now be oppressed, weakened and almost destroyed by your soldiers, just as it has so often been by other invaders in the past . . . Yet it will never be utterly exterminated by the wrath of Man, unless the wrath of God should strike it all the same time. Whatever else may happen, I do not believe that any other people but the Welsh, or any other than the Welsh language, will answer to the Supreme Judge on the Last Day for this corner of the earth'.

Gerald the Writer
by Brynley F. Roberts

Giraldus Cambrensis is known to us almost completely from his own writings. Educated in England and Paris and a respected canon lawyer and diplomatist, he nevertheless disliked court life which he believed fostered selfish ambition. Whenever his 'official' life weighed too heavily on his spirit he invariably retreated to the haven of the Schools — to Paris, Oxford, Hereford, Lincoln — where he could continue his studies and enjoy the tranquility which the contemplation of the higher, less transient life gave. When he retired from royal service in 1194 he seems to have spent some years in Lincoln where his skills as a hagiographer were put to good use and where he wrote some saints' Lives which are not in the conventional mould. More interestingly, as the reforming archdeacon of Brecon he produced for the clergy of St Davids *The Jewel of the Church*, a warm, personal handbook of moral exhortation.

But for all his mistrust of the standards of political life in court and church, he was no recluse. He relied on human contacts and on the world around him to satisfy his multifarious interests and to stimulate his energies. His years in royal service were not wasted, for what he observed at court and experienced on official tours of Ireland and Wales was to provide him with material for future books, as he tells us himself.

> 'Even when he followed the Court he nonetheless wrote histories, and after long and laborious journeys, such as are the lot of courtiers, would keep vigil till dawn, working by candlelight and joining night to day'.

The periods he spent in Ireland between 1183 and 1186, the tour of Wales in 1188, the tensions at the court between 1189 and 1194, were to produce *The Topography of Ireland* and *The Conquest of Ireland* (1188), *The Journey through Wales* (1191) and *The Description of Wales* (1194) perhaps the first version of *The Instruction of a Prince* (about 1194), and *The Life of Geoffrey Archbishop of York* (1193).

Gerald was a professional author, for ever making notes and setting down ideas to be developed in a future book, working to commissions but also resolving personal difficulties and finding relaxation in literary endeavours. Following his acceptance of defeat in his campaign for St Davids in 1203, between 1205 and 1218 he was to write three books which are not so much a record of the struggle as a personal vindication, his autobiography, *De Rebus a Se Gestis*, a

The popularity of Gerald's works through the ages: A fourteenth-century manuscript of the Journey through Wales, through to a recent paperback edition (By courtesy of the National Library of Wales).

collection of documents *(De Invectionibus)* and his final reflections *(De Jure et Statu Menevensis Ecclesiae)*. For all his education, Gerald was not an intellectual. He is better at reflecting ideas than originating them, more skilled in quoting authors than discussing them; but he is very consciously a writer and a stylist, constantly revising his work and producing new editions. He enjoys composing intricately wrought sentences, their clauses nicely balanced or paralleled. The tricks often appear to be too self-consciously contrived and he cannot pass up an opportunity for word-play, puns, etymologies, rhymes or alliteration. Having laboured over a rhetorical flourish or a well-turned sentence, he never hesitates to use them more than once. But he is a fluent writer, at his vivid, vivacious, anecdotal best when he presents a narrative, and in spite of an incorrigible tendency to digress, he has the historian's ability to structure his account of events so that it becomes a coherent narrative often enlivened by vignettes of the main protagonists. Gerald's interest was in men and in the world, in recent history and in nature: as a traveller he was excited by the exotic and the odd. But most of all he was interested in himself. He is at the centre of his best work, implicitly in the energy which stems from personal involvement in or emotional attachment to his theme, or explicitly in his autobiographical books. His personality, prejudices and opinions gave his writing the vitality which makes this medieval author so in accord with modern taste.

The Journey through Wales is, ostensibly, an account of the tour in 1188, but in reality the diary becomes the vehicle for Gerald's view of Wales. If the journey is the frame, the picture contains not only the day to day happenings but comments on the history, customs, people, natural history and politics of those parts of Wales Gerald knew best. In the tradition of the best travel books, the author's personality, more so than the events themselves, make the journey memorable. But the view lacked the coherent pattern a history demands. Having completed his *Journey*, Gerald used his training in composition to present a more generalized picture, *A Description of Wales*. This is his most carefully constructed work, symmetrical and balanced in its two parts, the one the antithesis of the other — the good and the bad points of the Welsh. Its brevity is a mark of its discipline, and its restrained, objective tone a sign of real contemplation. Gerald's Welsh books are those modern readers respond to most easily, because of the intrinsic interest of the subject matter and the warmth of Gerald's personality. But these first writings are not only the most interesting, they are also the best because they are the tautest in composition, the most general in appeal.

A twelfth-century scribe at work. From the Eadwine Psalter, produced at Christ Church, Canterbury, about 1150-60 (By courtesy of Trinity College, Cambridge, Ms. R 17 1, f.283v).

Gerald's Main Works

The list includes approximate dates of their first appearance, but no reference to second and third editions

1188	*Topographia Hibernica* The Topography of Ireland *Expugnatio Hibernica* The Conquest of Ireland
1191	*Itinerarium Kambriae* The Journey through Wales
1194	*Descriptio Kambriae* A Description of Wales *Vita Sancti Davidis* The Life of St David
1195	*Vita Galfridi Archiepiscopi Eboracensis* The Life of Geoffrey Archbishop of York
1197	*Gemma Ecclesiastica* The Jewel of the Church
1198	*Vita Sancti Remigii* The Life of St Remi
1208	*De Rebus a Se Gestis* Autobiography
1213	*Vita Sancti Hugonis* The Life of St Hugh
1216	*De Invectionibus* A Book of Invectives *Speculum Duorum* A Mirror of Two Men
1218	*De Jure et Statu Menevensis Ecclesiae* The Rights and Status of St Davids *De Principis Instructione* The Instruction of a Prince
1220	*Speculum Ecclesiae* The Mirror of the Church
Uncertain date	*Vita Sancti Ethelberti* The Life of St Ethelbert

Failure and Success
Gerald's Last Years and Ultimate Achievement

Gerald lived for twenty more years after abandoning his claim to St Davids in 1203: they were not years of contentment. He seems to have spent much of this time in Lincoln (where his contacts included his old Paris acquaintance and theology tutor, William de Monte) but to believe that he 'retired' there, or that he ever really retired at all, is to underestimate the indefatigable Gerald. He continued to write feverishly, and throughout his sixties he continued to travel, visiting his Irish relations in 1204-5 and in 1206 journeying on pilgrimage to Rome, where he renewed his friendship with Pope Innocent. He also returned to Wales at least three times, though his enthusiasm for the Welsh Church (and the Welsh people) had faded with his failure to win St Davids, whose Welsh canons he blamed for deserting his cause.

He soon developed a much more bitter grudge against his young nephew Gerald fitz Philip, son of his favourite brother. In 1203, by a

The effigy generally attributed to Gerald in St Davids Cathedral is more likely to be that of his disappointing nephew, Gerald fitz Philip. Gerald himself was probably buried at Lincoln.

Many of Gerald's books were widely read in the Middle Ages. One of the most popular was the Topography of Ireland (see pp.16-17), here translated into Provençal, the language of southern France (By permission of the British Library, Additional Ms. 17920, ff.26v-27).

convenient but highly irregular arrangement, Gerald had resigned his archdeaconry of Brecon to this nephew, while retaining the revenues of the office for himself. Five years later, however, young Gerald attempted to annex the revenues as well, thus seriously reducing old Gerald's income. The old man was deeply wounded by his ingratitude: had he not brought the boy up, supervised his education and lavished affection on him, calling him — a most surprising sidelight on Gerald's character — 'my little duckling'? And how did the wretched youth repay him? Not content with going disgracefully native (the nephew apparently preferred speaking Welsh to civilised French or Latin, and practising Welsh archery or the Welsh harp to sober theology) he ill-treated his uncle's horses, beat up his servants, and filched his rightful revenues.

His nephew's betrayal was only one of the disappointments which blighted Gerald's closing years, as they had beset his earlier life. There was talk (he claims) of making him bishop of Lincoln, or even a cardinal, but it all came to nothing, while the memory of St Davids brought only

pain. In 1207 (he alleges) King John urged him to renew the struggle for an independent Welsh archbishopric, but John had let him down before. Neither would he stand for election when St Davids became vacant in 1214, unless monarch, archbishop and every one of the canons backed him: 'which', he remarked cynically, 'would be nothing short of a miracle'.

Gerald's growing disillusion is reflected in his later books — bitter, querulous works for the most part, justifying his own actions and blaming his enemies for past setbacks. One of them is significantly named *Invectiones* ('Reproaches') and another, *Speculum Duorum* ('The Mirror of Two Men'), is a savage attack on his nephew, but probably the most scurrilous is *De Principis Instructione* ('On the Education of a Prince'), a vituperative denunciation of the Plantagenet kings (pp.18-21). Gerald, indeed, had come to hate his former masters, and in 1216 the old man enthusiastically welcomed the invading Prince Louis of France, called over by rebellious barons intent on destroying the English royal house. Better a French king, he argued, than a God-cursed Plantagenet. But once again he was doomed to disappointment, for in May 1217 a Plantagenet army routed the French and their allies at the very gates of Lincoln Cathedral. If Gerald was still living there, he may have witnessed his last hope shattered before his eyes. There was now nothing left for him but to 'indulge his love of books in his humble habitation, and weep for his sins in the corners of churches' — and to trust to posterity for the rewards he had been denied in life. He died in 1223 at the age of about seventy-seven: the whereabouts of his grave are unknown, but he was probably buried in Lincoln, far from the St Davids he had striven so hard to gain.

Though Gerald died a deeply disappointed man, he was right to trust in posterity. Perhaps his best

epitaph, indeed, was spoken by Archbishop Baldwin on the last day of their crusading mission to Wales. More than all the passing riches or perishable honours of this world, declared the prelate, Gerald should prize his gift for authorship — 'For his books could not pass away or perish, but the longer they lasted and the greater their antiquity, so to all future ages they would become more beloved and more precious'.

Baldwin spoke truly. In his own lifetime, even Gerald's popular books on Wales and Ireland enjoyed only a limited circulation: it could not be otherwise, since each copy had to be laboriously written out by hand. Not until their Latin texts were first printed in Elizabethan times did they become really well known, while the appearance of English and Welsh

translations from the nineteenth century onwards increased their popularity a hundredfold. There is no doubt at all, indeed, that Gerald's books are now read and appreciated by a far greater number of people than even he could ever have dreamt of. In the last analysis, then, the mixed Norman-Welsh descent that dogged his career with failure was also the root of his ultimate success. None but a man of Gerald's background and education, neither wholly a foreigner nor completely at home in the land of his birth, could have produced the mirror of medieval Wales he bequeathed us — a mirror which has indeed grown 'more beloved and more precious' over eight centuries.

Gerald seems to have spent much of his later life at Lincoln. There, between the late twelfth and early thirteenth centuries, the great cathedral was in a stage of major reconstruction (Photograph by David Robinson).

A Handlist of Exhibits at the Gerald of Wales Exhibition

compiled by J. M. Lewis

This handlist of manuscripts, church treasures, works of art and other objects is prepared on the occasion of the exhibition: *Gerald of Wales: The Crusading Priest,* organized by Cadw: Welsh Historic Monuments and held at the National Museum of Wales 23 March — 30 October 1988. The exhibits are arranged here in broad categories for easy reference. The list also serves as a record of this unique celebration, and the gathering together of these precious objects from many parts of Britain.

Manuscripts

Included first are two manuscripts that were probably among the books of the abbey of Gloucester during Gerald's time there. Also included, to illustrate the ancient culture of Wales, which formed part of his mixed heritage, are two of Wales's most celebrated medieval manuscripts: the Black Book of Carmarthen and the Law Book of Hywel Dda. To illustrate his importance as an author, copies of three of his many works are included: three copies of the *Topography of Ireland* (one a translation into Provençal), two of the *Description of Wales* and the only surviving manuscript of his *Life of St David.* It is interesting to note that three of the books exhibited (nos. 3, 5 and 8) belonged to the same library: that of St Augustine's Abbey, Canterbury.

1. Leaf from an 11th-cent. Ms.
Gloucester Cathedral Library

Part of an Anglo-Saxon translation of the *Rule of St Benedict,* under whose discipline the abbey of Gloucester operated, beginning: *Aerest mon seal god lufian of ealre heortan . . .* (First, one must love God with all one's heart . . .)

S. Eward, *Catalogue of the literary MSS in the Gloucester Cathedral Library,* Ms. 35.
N. R. Ker, *Catalogue of MSS containing Anglo-Saxon,* no.117.

2. Pseudo-Athanasius
Gloucester Cathedral Library

12th-century copy of a theological work refuting the Arian heresy (which claimed that Christ was not of the same nature as God).

S. Eward, *ibid.,* Ms. 2.

3. The Law Book of Hywel Dda
National Library of Wales, Ms. Peniarth 28

The most celebrated Latin text of the native laws of Wales, codified in the 10th cent. under the direction of Hywel Dda (the Good), copied somewhere in south Wales in the mid-13th century. Appropriate miniatures are used to mark significant places in the finely written text: open at ff. 5v-6, in the section of the work dealing with the officials of the royal court, their entitlements, rights and the fines payable if they are wronged. The illustrations represent The Doorkeeper and Porter, and the Chief Groom, the Cook and the Smith. The manuscript once belonged to St Augustine's Abbey, Canterbury, and may have been the copy used by Archbishop Peckham (1279-92).

H. D. Emanuel, *The Latin Texts of the Welsh Laws.*
NLWJ 19 (1975-76), 340-44.

4. The Black Book of Carmarthen (*Llyfr Du Caerfyrddin*)
National Library of Wales Ms. Peniarth 1

An important collection of early Welsh poetry, possibly copied by a scribe at the Augustinian priory of St John the Evangelist at Carmarthen. It consists of a collection of separate manuscripts bound together, and seems to be mainly the work of the same copyist at various times in his life. Mid-13th cent.

5. Gerald of Wales, *Topography of Ireland*
British Library Ms. Royal 13 B.VIII

This volume, which once belonged to St Augustine's Abbey Canterbury, includes the best known copies of three of Gerald's works. It is decorated with marginal illustrations (perhaps based on sketches in Gerald's own autograph copy), which make it a notable early example of the illustrated chronicle. Those shown (ff. 28v.-29) illustrate the killing of the mare, the bath in the stew of its meat and the eating of it (relating to the account of the method of confirming kingship in Tirconnel), two men of Connaught in a coracle, and an Irishman riding bare-chested on a horse. End of 12th-beginning of 13th-cent.

N. J. Morgan, *Early Gothic Manuscripts I 1190-1250, no.59a.*

6. Gerald of Wales, *Topography of Ireland*
British Library Ms. Harley 3724

This 13th-cent. manuscript was probably written in Ireland, and includes boldly coloured geometric panels and borders in the earlier tradition of Irish book illustration, but also naturalistic animal figures in a more contemporary style. The page exhibited (ff. 40v.-41) contains a lively drawing of a hare.

7. Gerald of Wales, *Topography of Ireland*
British Library Ms. Additional 17920

14th-cent. collection of works in Provençal, including a translation of the abridgement of the *Topography of Ireland* made by Philip, prior of the Dominican friary at Cork.

J. Ulrich, *Frère Philippe: Les merveilles d'Irlande.*

8. Gerald of Wales, *Description of Wales*
British Library Ms. Cotton Domitian 1

This 13th-cent. Ms. contains the earliest surviving copy of Gerald's *Description* and *Itinerary through Wales,* as well as an important copy of the earliest Welsh chronicle, the *Annales Cambriae* and other works relating to Wales. Open at ff. 58v.-59, showing decorated capitals. This book belonged to Dr John Dee, the 16th-cent. mathematician and astrologer, but before that part of it at least had belonged to St Augustine's Abbey Canterbury (as did nos.3 and 5).

9. Gerald of Wales, *Description of Wales*
British Library Ms. Cotton Vitellius C.10

This volume begins with a 14th-cent. copy of Gerald's *Description of Wales,* followed by later transcriptions of various documents relating to the country.

10. Gerald of Wales, *Life of St David*
British Library Ms. Royal 13 C 1

The only surviving manuscript of Gerald's *Life of St David,* copied *c.*1453-59 by the traveller and chronicler William Worcester while secretary to Sir John Fastolf. The volume includes several other historical works, including a life of Henry V, with whom Sir John had fought with distinction at Agincourt. Open at ff. 171v.,172, begining: *Beatus David ingenuis natalibus ortus . .* (The blessed David, born of noble parentage . . .).

Church Treasures

With the possible exception of the St Davids rings, these notable objects belong substantially to Gerald's lifetime, exemplifying some of the ecclesiastical forms and styles of decoration he would have been familiar with; the St Davids croziers he might even have known. In Britain the survival of church treasures must always be regarded as a lucky accident, in view of the confiscation and deliberate destruction to which objects have been subjected over the centuries. Even in times when their use was permitted, they were always liable to be recast or remodelled according to current fashion. This makes the survival of complete objects from the twelfth century remarkable in itself. Bishops' croziers and rings sometimes survive through being buried with their owners, as in the case of the splendid group from St Davids. The medieval provenance of the Monmouth crucifix, discovered in 1981, is not known, nor that of the liturgical comb, said to have been discovered in Wales.

11. Liturgical comb
British Museum, 1856, 6-23, 29

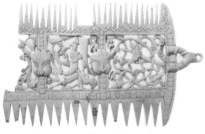

No. 11 (By permission of the British Museum).

Late 11th- or early 12th-cent. comb of walrus ivory. Combs were used by bishops to dress their hair before celebrating Mass, and were for centuries included among their ceremonial ornaments. This one is reputed to have been found in Wales. It has a double row of teeth and a loop for suspension. The central area is divided into three panels of open-work decoration, largely formal scroll-work, but with the central panel including the figure of a prostrate man attempting to push away the spear and shield of a helmeted warrior above him. Above the teeth on one side is a Latin

inscription: *. . .VD.VVLT.D...DEVS.IHC.XPS.* Neither this nor the scene have been satisfactorily interpreted.

ERA, no.184
J. Beckwith, *Ivory carvings in Early Medieval England,* no.47.

12. The Monmouth Crucifix
The Trustees of the Archdiocese of Cardiff
National Museum of Wales

Lacking only the base into which it fitted, this is one of only two complete English altar crosses to survive from the period. It is of gilt copper-alloy, richly moulded and decorated. The ends of the arms are enriched with settings containing semi-precious stones: the three milky-blue opals are replacements, but at the base the Roman onyx cameo of the head of Medusa may be original, an example of the not infrequent use of classical cameos in medieval work. The back is engraved with the Lamb of God and the four Evangelist symbols. The crowned figure of Christ is a finely detailed and expressive work. *c.* 1170-80.

ERA, no. 241.

13. Top of a crozier
St Davids Cathedral

Gilt copper-alloy. The crook, decorated with open-work foliage, the upper knop and the bands probably date from the mid-12th century. The lower knop belongs to the 13th century, when the three sections were assembled. Found in 1865-6 (with ring no.18A) in a bishop's grave in front of the *pulpitum,* probably that of Bishop Richard de Carew (d.1280).

ERA no.268
Arch. Camb. 1866, 61.

14. Fragments of a crozier
St Davids Cathedral

Gilt copper-alloy. The crook is decorated with a foliage design developing into a central 'orchid' blossom. The fragment of wooden shaft has a richly decorated mount including the upper part of a spherical knop that has broken away. *c.* 1150-80. Found in 1844 in the grave of a bishop on the south side of the presbytery.

ERA no.270
W. B. Jones & E. A. Freeman, *The History and Antiquities of St Davids,* 113.

No. 14 (Photograph courtesy of the National Museum of Wales).

15. Part of the crook of a crozier
St Davids Cathedral

Gilt copper-alloy. The design consists of an eagle encircled by a branch springing into bud. This made up the inner scroll of decoration round which an outer scroll would have fitted. Similarities of style to work at Wells, Glastonbury and Llandaff have suggested that it was made in a West Country workshop. *c.* 1180-1200. Found in 1865-6 (with ring no.18B) in a grave in front of the *pulpitum,* perhaps that of Bishop Thomas Bek (1280-93).

ERA no.273
Arch. Camb. 1866, 62.

16. Bishop's ring
British Museum 1885, 6-15,1

Gold, with stirrup-shaped hoop rising to a pointed bezel set with an irregular six-sided sapphire. Similar to two rings from bishops' tombs at Chichester. Mid-12th cent. Found at Wittersham, Kent.

ERA, no.315

17. Bishop's ring
British Museum 1925, 1-13, 1

No. 17 (By permission of the British Museum).

Gold, with highly decorated hoop inscribed AVE MARIA GRA/TIA PLENA DMI (Hail Mary full of the grace of the Lord). Oval bezel with open-work decoration of birds, set with an uncut sapphire. Late 12th-early 13th cent. Found in 1924 at Cannington, Somerset.

ERA, no.317
Antiq.J. 1925, 278-9.

18. Two bishop's rings
St Davids Cathedral

A. Gold, with plain cylindrical hoop and elongated octagonal bezel containing an uncut rose-coloured gem. Found with crozier no.13.

B. Gold, with plain hoop and pear-shaped bezel containing an uncut oval gem, probably an amethyst, held by four claws. Found with crozier no.15.

Arch. Camb. 1866, 61-2.
Archaeologia 60.2 (1907), 489 and 491.

Jewellery and Objets d'Art

19. The Lewis Chessmen
British Museum 1831, 11-1, nos 1, 7, 16 & 38

No. 19, king (left), queen (right) (By permission of the British Museum).

Four walrus-ivory chessmen — a king, queen, bishop and knight — from the cache of 78 such pieces found in 1831 in a stone chamber in a sand dune near the shore of the Isle of Lewis, Outer Hebrides. They could be of Scandinavian or English manufacture, and may have formed part of the cargo of a wrecked merchant ship. Mid-late 12th cent.

ERA, no.212
J. Becwith, *Ivory Carving in Early Medieval England,* no.166.

20. Six silver finger rings
British Museum 1854, 8-20, 1-6

Part of a hoard dated to 1173-4, found at Lark Hill near Worcester in 1853. The rings illustrate types fashionable among the less wealthy at the time: (a) three with rectangular bezels — one set with a crystal backed by red foil, one with an amethyst and one with yellow paste; (b) a ring made of two wires twisted together, a type known from the Viking and late Anglo-Saxon period; (c) a ring with a bezel consisting of three panels decorated with cross motifs.

ERA, no.320.
Archaeologia 1855, pl.xvii.

No. 16 (centre) and No. 20 (By permission of the British Museum).

21. Bronze finger ring
Cadw: Welsh Historic Monuments

Rectangular bezel with oval recess, its convex base tinned to light a clear stone, which is missing. 12th-13th cent. Excavated at Laugharne Castle, Dyfed.

22. Gilt bronze mounts
Cadw: Welsh Historic Monuments

Perhaps for decorating the cover of a wooden box. 13th cent. Laugharne Castle, Dyfed.

23. Bone mount
Cadw: Welsh Historic Monuments

Carved strip decorated with incised ring-and-dot design, with nail holes for attachment, perhaps to a wooden box, or casket. 13th cent. Laugharne Castle, Dyfed.

Stone Sculpture

24. The 'Conbelin Stone' (cast)
National Museum of Wales

Sculptured cross from Margam, West Glamorgan, an important pre-Norman religious centre. Late 9th-early 10th cent.

RCAHM *Glamorgan Inventory* Vol.1, Part 3, no.907.

25. Grotesque head
Gloucester Cathedral

Label-stop (terminating a moulding) or arch-stone from a small opening, in the form of a monster with furrowed brow and elongated ears. 12th cent.

26. Head of an angel
Hereford Cathedral

Probably from the west front of the cathedral, which collapsed in 1786. 13th-14th cent.

27. Head of a knight
Cadw: Welsh Historic Monuments

No. 27.

Found in the chapter house at Haverfordwest Priory during recent excavations. The effigy of which this was part probably marked the grave of an important early benefactor. He is represented wearing a hood (or *coif*), which would have been attached to a *hauberk* or shirt of mail, the type of armour being worn by the figures on some of the seals (nos.30-31). Probably mid-13th cent.

28. Crowned head
Lord Mostyn
(National Museum of Wales 77.11H)

Decorated corbel of the mid-13th cent. found at Deganwy Castle and probably belonging to the castle of Llywelyn the Great (see no.30).

Antiq.J., 1967, 112.
Archaeol.J., 1967, 197.

29. Capital with crowned heads.
Cadw: Welsh Historic Monuments

Found in the chapter house at Haverfordwest Priory during recent excavations. Intended to support the springing of an elaborate vault, this remarkable work consists of seven conjoined heads — the end ones in profile, the rest carved in the round — sharing between them six eyes in such a way that each head is completely represented. Late 14th cent.

Seals

The seals of the Welsh lords and princes follow the same design as their Norman counterparts, normally carrying an image of a knight on horseback. Each wears a chain-mail *hauberk,* a surcoat, and a round-topped helmet with protection for the nose, and carries a shield slung by a strap over the right shoulder and a scabbard at the waist; the raised right hand holds a sword.

30. Gwenwynwyn ap Owain Cyfeiliog, Lord of Powys (d.1216)
Wynnstay Collection
National Library of Wales

NLWJ 23 (1983-4), 302 (no.IX.2)

31. Morgan ap Caradog and his brother Cadwallon
British Library Harley Charter 75 B.29

Morgan, Lord of Avan in Glamorgan, accompanied the party of 1188 through his lordship, guiding them (not very successfully) round the treacherous quicksands of the Neath estuary; Caradog held the lordship of Glynrhondda. Their seals are attached to a charter confirming a gift of land at Pendar in upland Glamorgan to the Cistercian order of monks.

British Museum Seal Cat. nos.5946 and 5944.
NLWJ 23 (1983-4), 298-9 (nos.I.1 and II).

32. William Saltmarsh, Bishop of Llandaff, 1186-91
National Museum of Wales 44.171

Seal and counter-seal (casts). The seal depicts a bishop in Mass vestments. The counter seal appears to be the impression of an early Christian gem, with a tall cross between two male heads facing each other.
Gerald describes him as 'that good and honest man'. He accompanied the party of 1188 through his diocese, entertained them at Llandaff, and preached there with the archbishop. On his death in 1191, the diocese was offered to Gerald, who declined it.

Arch. Camb. 1984, 116 nos.28 and 30.

Coins

33. Short-cross pennies struck at Rhuddlan between 1180 and 1215
National Museum of Wales E 1076, 1080, 1086, 1088-90, 1092

No. 33 (By courtesy of the National Museum of Wales).

The 'short cross' silver penny was introduced by Henry II in 1180. It was produced as the sole English coin type at mints throughout the country until 1247, always in the name *Henricus Rex*. Locally mined silver was coined at Rhuddlan successively by the moneyers Halli, Tomas, Simond, and Henricus between about 1180 and 1215. A coin struck by Simond (*c.* 1205-10) is illustrated (NMW E 1086):

Ob. *HENRICVS.REX* Stylised portrait with sceptre;
Rev. *SIMOND.ON.RVLA* Short cross with crosslets in the angles.

Household Objects

34. Brass mortar
National Museum of Wales 82.24H

An Islamic form of pharmaceutical mortar, possibly 12th cent. in date, which may have

No. 34 (By courtesy of the National Museum of Wales).

been brought back from a Crusade. Coity Castle, Mid Glamorgan.

Antiq.J. 64 (1984), 324-6.

35. Pottery tripod-pitcher
National Museum of Wales 1986.95H

Loughor Castle, West Glamorgan. *c.* 1220

MPMW, no.4.

36. Pottery costrel
National Museum of Wales 64.51/3

No. 36 (By courtesy of the National Museum of Wales).

Such vessels, slung over the shoulder or hanging from a belt, were used by travellers to carry liquid refreshment. Pottery forms sometimes, as in this case, imitate wooden casks. Cardiff Castle.

MPMW, no.8.
Trans. Cardiff Naturalists' Soc. 93 (1964-66), 40.

37. Wooden bucket
National Museum of Wales 53.123

No. 37 (By courtesy of the National Museum of Wales).

From the well at Castell-y-bere, Gwynedd. Reconstructed.

Arch. Camb. 1974, 100-1.

38. Knife-blade and tang
Cadw: Welsh Historic Monuments

Laugharne Castle, Dyfed

39. Scissors
National Museum of Wales 40.226

Criccieth Castle, Gwynedd.

Arch. Camb. 1944-5, 41

40. Stone spindle whorl
Cadw: Welsh Historic Monuments

Used as a fly-wheel on the spindle when spinning wool. Laugharne Castle, Dyfed.

41. Barrel padlock and key
Cadw: Welsh Historic Monuments

A type of lock in which the spring was depressed by *pushing in* and not *turning* the key. Laugharne Castle, Dyfed

42. Chest key
Cadw: Welsh Historic Monuments

Decorated with bands of inlay, probably of tin. Laugharne Castle, Dyfed.

Objects for leisure & amusement

43. Bone flute
National Museum of Wales 32. 429/12

End blown flute or flageolet (blown like a recorder or 'tin whistle') made from the leg bone of a red deer. Suitable for accompanying the solo singing of a minstrel rather than the part-singing that Gerald mentions. 13th cent. White Castle, Gwent.

Medieval Archaeology 5(1961), 176-80.

44. Bone whistle
Cadw: Welsh Historic Monuments

No. 44 (Photograph by Richard Avent).

Laugharne Castle, Dyfed.

45. Bone chessman
National Museum of Wales 67.409

Skenfrith Castle, Gwent.

No. 45 (left), No. 46 (right) (By courtesy of the National Museum of Wales).

46. Ivory chessman (pawn)
National Museum of Wales 31 78/37

Caerleon Castle, Gwent

J. E. Lee, *Isca,* pl.30,15.

47. Five gaming pieces
National Museum of Wales 49.427 and 31.78
Cadw: Welsh Historic Monuments

For playing board-games of the Nine-Men's-Morris type.

A. Rûg Castle, Gwynedd.
RCHM *Merioneth Inventory,* no.38.

B. Caerleon, Gwent.
J. E. Lee, *Isca,* pl.30,16.

C. Laugharne Castle, Dyfed.

No. 47C (Photograph by Richard Avent).

Horse-furniture.

48. Three prick-spurs
National Museum of Wales 1986.95H
Cadw: Welsh Historic Monuments

The form of spur in use until it was superseded by the more familiar rowel-spur in the 14th cent. Loughor Castle, West Glamorgan and Laugharne Castle, Dyfed.

49. Horse Shoe
National Museum of Wales 40.244

Criccieth Castle, Gwynedd.

Arch. Camb. 1944-5, 41.

50. Horse bit
National Museum of Wales 40.224

Criccieth Castle, Gwynedd.

Arch. Camb. 1944-5, 41.

Military Objects

While the knight fought with sword and lance, the common soldier of the Middle Ages used a spear or a bow. The arrowheads exhibited include the long, armour-piercing type as well as the broad-bladed form used against the more lightly protected; the heavier conical bolt-heads were used with the more powerful crossbow.

51. Spearhead
Cadw: Welsh Historic Monuments

Laugharne Castle, Dyfed.

52. Three arrowheads and two crossbow bolts
Cadw: Welsh Historic Monuments

Laugharne Castle, Dyfed.

Abbreviations

Antiq.J.   *Antiquaries Journal*
Arch. Camb. *Archaeologia Cambrensis*
Arch.J.   *Archaeological Journal*
ERA   *English Romanesque Art 1066-1200* (Arts Council 1984)
MPMW   *Medieval Pottery and Metalware in Wales* (National Museum of Wales 1978)
NLWJ   *National Library of Wales Journal*
RCAHM   *Royal Commission on Ancient & Historic Monuments (Wales)*